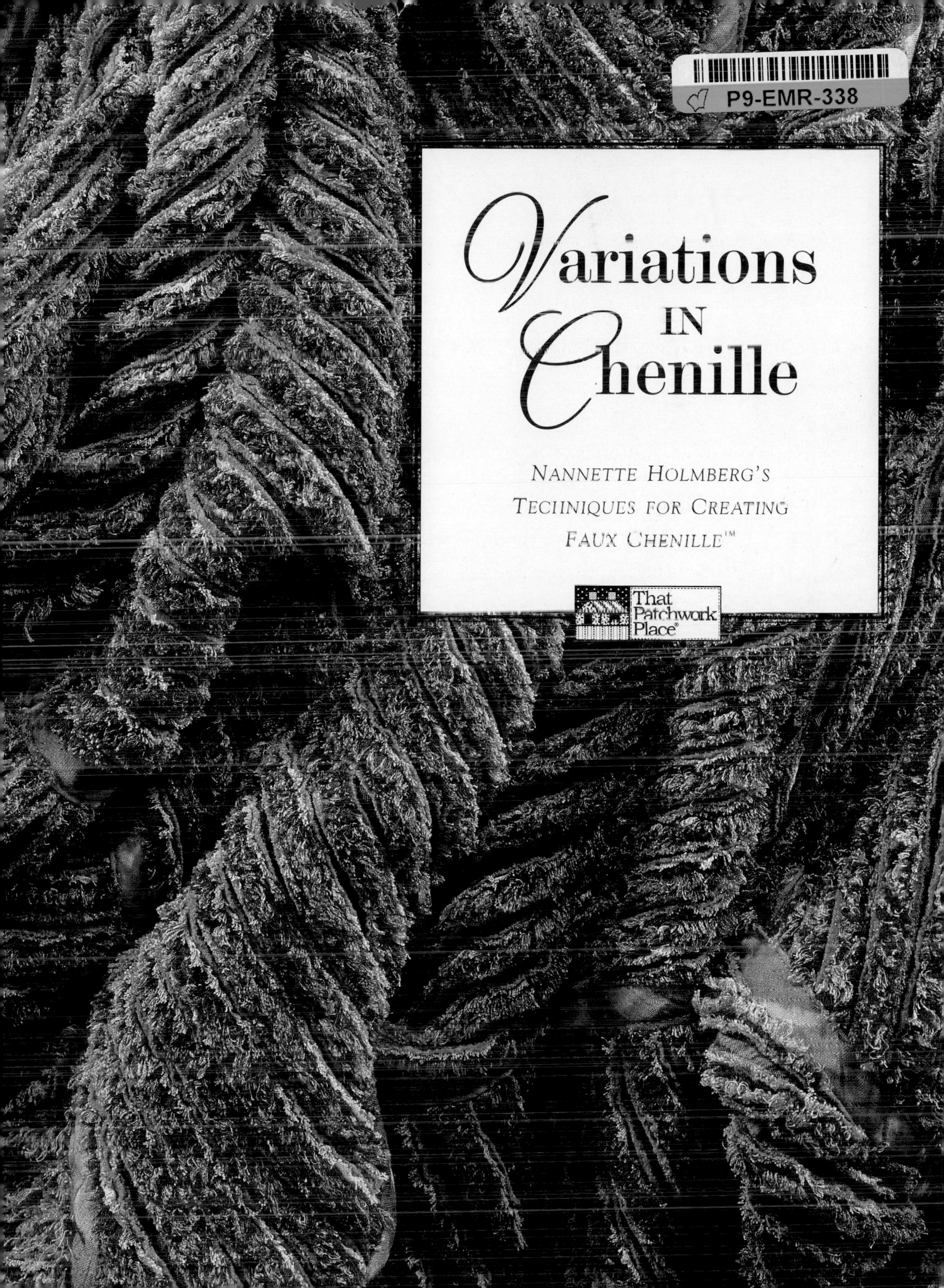

P9-EMR-338
Variations in Chenille
Nannette Holmberg's
Techniques for Creating
Faux Chenille™
That Patchwork Place®

Acknowledgments

Thanks to:

Virginia Lewis Richardson, who encouraged a young college student to become a designer.

Lucille Graham, who created works of art and inspired me to learn.

Kathleen Deneris, who inspired me and encouraged me to explore.

The members of the Salt Lake City Surface Design Group, for their creativity and eagerness to share.

The talented designers who were willing to share their remarkable works in this book.

Bernina of America and Springs Industries, for their fine products.

Special thanks to:

Linda Zarchin, for her generosity, encouragement, support, and elegant rayons, but most of all for her friendship.

My editor, Laura Munson Reinstatler, for her friendship, enthusiasm, and cheerful support that made this book possible.

The entire staff at That Patchwork Place, who do the magic and turn dreams into reality.

Dedication

To my ever-patient husband, David;
to my beautiful and talented daughter, Erin;
to my multi-talented mother, Mollie Jackstien Barlow, who taught me to sew and to pursue my dreams;
and in loving memory of my father, LaVerl "Bud" Barlow, who made me realize that I could indeed reach up and touch the stars.

Credits

Editor-in-Chief — Kerry I. Smith
Technical Editor — Laura M. Reinstatler
Managing Editor — Judy Petry
Copy Editor — Tina Cook
Proofreader — Leslie Phillips
Design Director — Cheryl Stevenson
Cover Designer — Trina Stahl
Text Designer — Kay Green
Design Assistant — Marijane E. Figg
Illustrator — Robin Strobel
Photographer — Brent Kane

MISSION STATEMENT

We are dedicated to providing quality products and service by working together to inspire creativity and to enrich the lives we touch.

Variations in Chenille: Nannette Holmberg's Techniques for Creating Faux Chenille™

Martingale & Company, PO Box 118
Bothell, WA 98041-0118 USA

Printed in Hong Kong
02 01 00 99 98 97 6 5 4 3 2 1

Library of Congress Cataloging-in-Publication Data

Holmberg, Nannette,
Variations in chenille : Nannette Holmberg's techniques for creating faux chenille.
p. cm.
ISBN 1-56477-206-3
1. Patchwork. 2. Quilted goods. 3. Tufted textiles. 4. Novelty fabrics. I. title.
TT835. H55623 1997
746.46—dc21 97-27636
CIP

Contents

Introduction

Every artist searches for a medium in which to express aesthetic ideas. A few artists know from the beginning the best means for conveying their message and make it their life's work. Others think they know the appropriate medium and pursue it for years before realizing there could be more. I fall in the latter category.

Anything to do with sewing and fabrics fascinated me from the time I was a small child. If I could be at the sewing machine with my mother, I was happy. Although I did well at my studies in high school, I preferred to sew. By the time I entered college, my interest in any other subject had completely disappeared, and I found myself cutting other classes to work on my sewing-construction class projects. When my professor—who was also the head of the fashion-design department—suggested I consider fashion design as a major, I had no hesitation.

After college, fashion design seemed to be the right choice, but I always felt I wanted to do more. As I collaborated over the years with several artists, I found I loved combining their artistic expression with my work. Lucille Graham's elegant machine embroidery, combined with my fashion design, was a natural collaboration that began more than twenty-five years ago. I watched in awe as Lucille wrote beautiful books on machine embroidery and shared her talents.

About the same time, I began working with fiber artist Douglas Ram Samuj. Douglas's use of color and intricately printed fabrics was an inspiration. Although my business focused on bridal and evening wear, I was fascinated with the work of my associates.

Wanting to explore more techniques and possibilities, I first attended a workshop to become an instructor of machine-embroidery techniques. More workshops followed. Each new technique opened doors and created exciting possibilities, revealing new ways to use up twenty-five years of accumulated fabrics, laces, and trims. "You'll never use it all," my father used to say.

In the meantime, I made wedding gowns, hundreds of them. At the same time, I pursued my interest in wearable art, which changed constantly. Every technique I had learned over the years became part of my collection, and the bridal and wearable-art styles often merged.

As I explored these new methods, I saw garments made by a process called *slashing*. This popular technique involved layering 100% cottons, then machine stitching the layers together in rows or small squares. After completing the stitching, the layers were cut (slashed) and washed several times until they "did something," meaning that the edges frayed. Some called the effect "blooming." I called it disappointing. The results were frequently stiff, rough, and unattractive. There appeared to be limited uses for this look and procedure.

During and after slashing's brief period of popularity, not much was written about it. At first I believed this was because the method offered little in the way of possibilities, yet I heard a great deal about a designer by the name of Tim Harding who had been successfully using this technique for years. What did he know that I didn't?

Several years ago, while attending a week-long retreat that presented many interesting projects, I was reintroduced to slashing. This time, however, the fabrics used were a combination of cottons and 100% rayon (that "unwashable" fabric). Layering cotton and rayon seemed to bring the resulting fabric to life and gave it a soft, rich texture. This time I was fascinated with the possibilities.

The soft, textured, cut-edge-finished jacket I completed in this class was inspiring. I was like a sculptor discovering clay. Upon my return home, I began to play with the technique and explore its possibilities. My original projects were basic, with all the seams and edges left unfinished. Although the look was interesting, I wanted to add more finishing detail to my jackets. Because of the custom design work I was known for, I wanted to offer my customers more of a high-fashion, couture finish to these textured jackets.

Logic told me that because these jackets were washed in a washing machine and dried in a dryer, and because of the shrinkage that occurred in the process, I would need to be careful about detail and finishing work. So I started slowly, taking few risks. My first vests had simple raw-edged bindings and bound seams.

seemed appropriate because it didn't describe the luxurious look of the finished fabric. And "blooming" wasn't right either. After considering many new terms and clever phrases, I decided that this soft, textured fabric reminded me of the old faded bedspread from my youth. I have called the fabrics that I create by this process Faux Chenille™ ever since.

Making these jackets has consumed my life. When I finish a jacket, I find new ideas for the next one, and the next. My file of sketches and ideas is full of future projects. I sincerely hope the following pages will inspire you to make projects you never dreamed you could create.

Let's begin to create variations in chenille.

I washed the vests and dried them. They looked great! The bindings didn't pull or distort. I used bias trim to divide design areas on my jackets. It worked! I finished all the edges of my jackets with detailed bias bindings and topstitching. Everything went through the entire slashing process like a dream. From this I moved on to a series of experiments with all types of bindings, ribbons, and trims. Much to my amazement, everything I tried succeeded.

I asked myself, "If I had this kind of success with trims, what would happen if I experimented with fabric combinations?" I played with more rayons. The resulting jackets had the soft drape of fine silk. I pulled everything imaginable out of my fabric stash, trying cottons, silks, woolens, laces and more, making sample blocks from different combinations. After each sample I became more excited and thought, "What if?"

The jackets I began to create were truly one-of-a-kind originals. I found that the colorations and textures created by each combination of fabrics could not be duplicated. Even when using the same fabrics, changing the order in which they were stacked gave completely different results. It was fun and infectious. I couldn't stop.

Soon I decided that the soft, textured fabric created with this technique had a new look and should have a new name. "Slashing" no longer

The Recipe

I like to think that creating chenille is as simple as following a recipe. A successful chenille fabric is the result of a successful combination of "ingredients." The right ingredients, when combined in the proper manner and order, produce a fabric with a soft, rich texture that is a pleasure to wear. If the ingredients don't work well together or are assembled in an improper order, the results will be disappointing; the "cake" will flop.

After years of trial and error, failure and success, I've come up with recipes that will help you avoid the chenille pitfalls. Creating chenille is not an exact science. I can't tell you to combine five or six layers of 100% cotton or 100% rayon and expect that you will have the same beautiful chenille that you see in this book. It isn't quite that easy, but it is fun getting there. You must have an adventurous spirit and be willing to spend some time exploring possibilities.

Approach chenille with an open mind. Try not to have a preconceived notion of what your final combination of fabrics will be. On some occasions your preliminary ideas may prove successful, but more often than not, you'll find yourself rearranging layers and adding or deleting fabrics in your sample stack until suddenly something works. It's good to be prepared for some combinations of fabrics that simply won't succeed as chenille no matter what you do to them.

General Supplies

Making chenille doesn't require purchasing a lot of supplies or tools if you have a few basics on hand. In addition to basic sewing supplies, you'll need the following:

- A sewing machine in good working order with an even straight stitch. It is helpful to have a zigzag stitch if you wish to add a decorative touch to the trims.
- Pins, pins, and more pins to hold the fabric layers together as you work. It's much easier to stitch and manipulate fabrics when they are pinned securely around the edges and about every three or four inches across the body of the piece. Pinning the layers helps avoid slippage and movement as you sew.
- A rotary cutter and cutting mat. These are especially helpful for trimming the uneven edges of pieces that have been layered, stitched, and slashed.
- A 6" x 24" or similar size clear acrylic ruler with a 45°-angle line to use as a marking guide. The 45°-angle line is essential for marking the stitching lines.
- A 6" or 8" Bias Square® or other square ruler.
- A marking tool such as tailor's chalk or washout-ink pens for marking the stitching lines. You also need a marking pencil or a waxy marker that will not rub off for areas such as the center back (where you need to see clearly the pivot-point line for chevron designs). Tailor's chalk tends to rub off quickly and requires continuous re-marking. Tailor's wax or a sliver of hand soap work better.
- Blunt-nosed scissors work best for slashing the layers. After you've spent so much time (and possibly money), you won't want to have any accidents while cutting the top layers of fabric. I use a pair of 8" bent-handled Gingher shears with blunt-nosed blades, which are less likely to puncture or cut the base fabric than sharp-pointed dressmaker's shears.

Optional

- A walking foot allows the top and bottom fabric layers to feed through the sewing machine at the same rate, reducing shifting and puckering. It is useful when you're working with slippery rayons or other soft fabrics. You can find a walking foot for almost any machine. If you don't have one, when you stitch fabric layers together, alternate the stitching direction for each row instead of beginning at the same edge each time.

- A quilting foot has a guide that can be set to several widths to help you stitch rows a consistent distance apart. The drawback to this attachment is that you may need to sew on the same side of each row of stitching.

Note. If you have trouble sewing quilting rows a consistent width apart, cut a strip of heavy paper (about the weight of poster board) to the width you desire and about 20" long. Place the strip next to the previous row of stitching and use it as a guide for the next row. Stitch right next to the edge for perfectly spaced rows.

- A basting gun, such as the QuilTak, "shoots" little plastic tabs into fabric to hold layers together, eliminating the need for pins. Many of my students have found this tool helpful.

Fabric Combinations

You'll need to search for and look at fabrics in a new way. To create successful chenille, you don't select fabric combinations the way you might for a quilt. Beautifully coordinating print and color combinations with comparable finishes and textures usually don't work for this technique. For chenille, combining fabrics that are totally unrelated in both color and texture often creates the most exciting results.

Make a game of it. Remembering to keep an open mind, begin by selecting some of those fabrics in your stash that haven't seen the light of day in twenty years. Fabrics that you tried to sell ten years ago at a garage sale for twenty-five cents a yard—fabrics no one would even look at—are excellent candidates for chenille. Now is the time to pull these fabrics out and experiment with them before you buy twelve or more yards of expensive fabrics. That way, you won't be as disappointed if your stash fabrics don't work, and you'll be thrilled if they do.

I've found that 100% natural fibers such as cotton, linen, and silk are excellent candidates for chenille. Even fine woolens layered in combination with other fibers can be interesting.

I ignore labels that proclaim "dry clean only" and suggest you do the same. These labels might discourage you from using a fabric to its full potential.

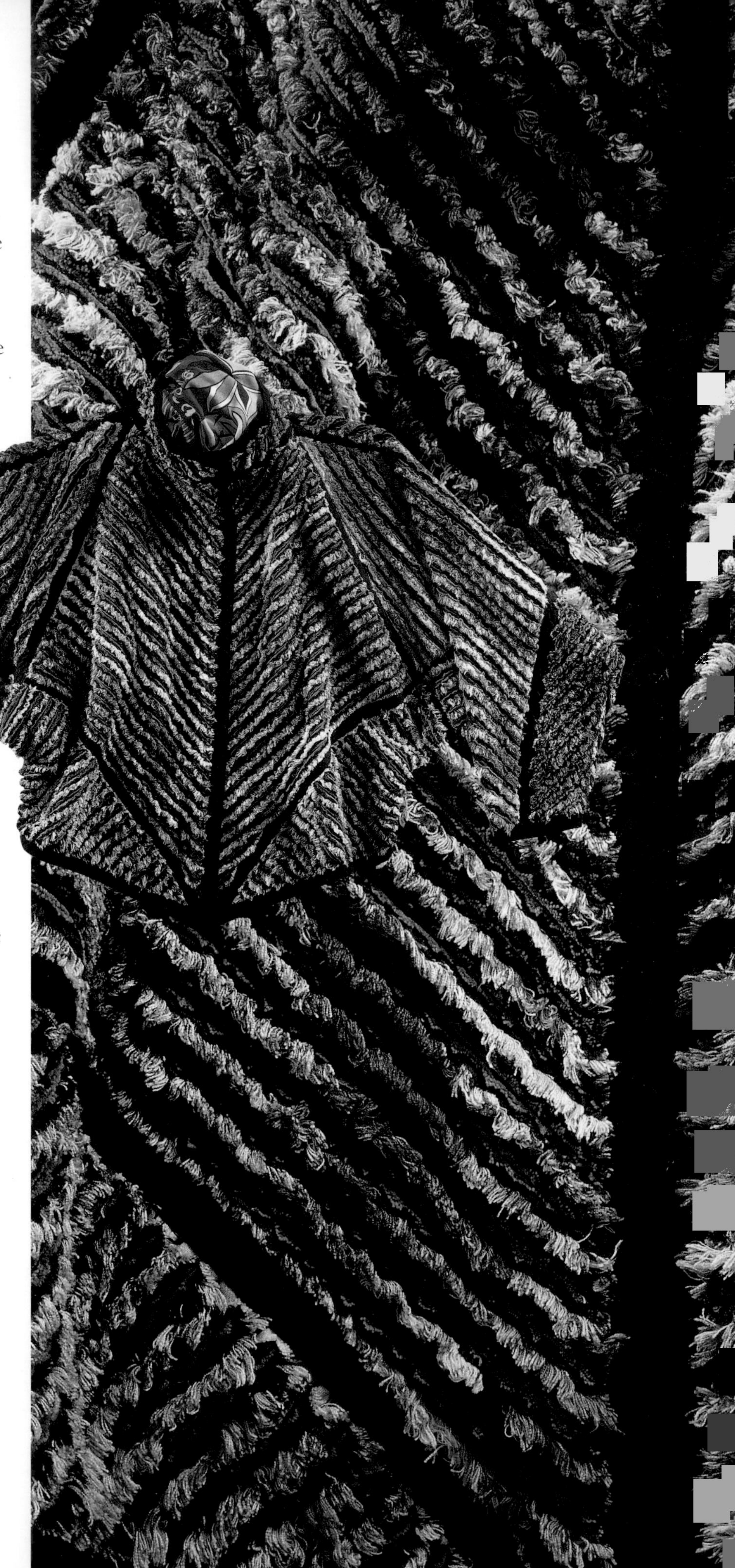

On the Bias Jacket

by Nannette Barlow Holmberg
When used as the top layer with other rayons, the "obnoxious" fabric shown on the previous page (lower right) becomes a beautiful sample block and a gorgeous jacket.

Silk

Silks layered by themselves often lie flat and lifeless after washing. Silks work best when layered with other fibers and textures. A few roughly textured, loosely woven silks and raw silks—when combined with loosely woven homespun cottons—can produce chenille with the look of rich fur.

Layers of silk, when used without fabrics made from other fibers, produce flat, dull chenille. The sample at left has not yet been laundered, while the one at right has. I experimented with stitching the slashed layers in different directions. While it creates an interesting look, it isn't successful chenille.

Layers of silk, homespun cotton, and rayon resemble a short, dense fur. Textured silks don't work well for the base, or lining, layer of chenille. Cotton broadcloth or soft rayon gives the finished garment the best hand (the best drape and feel to the touch) and provides the most comfort when worn.

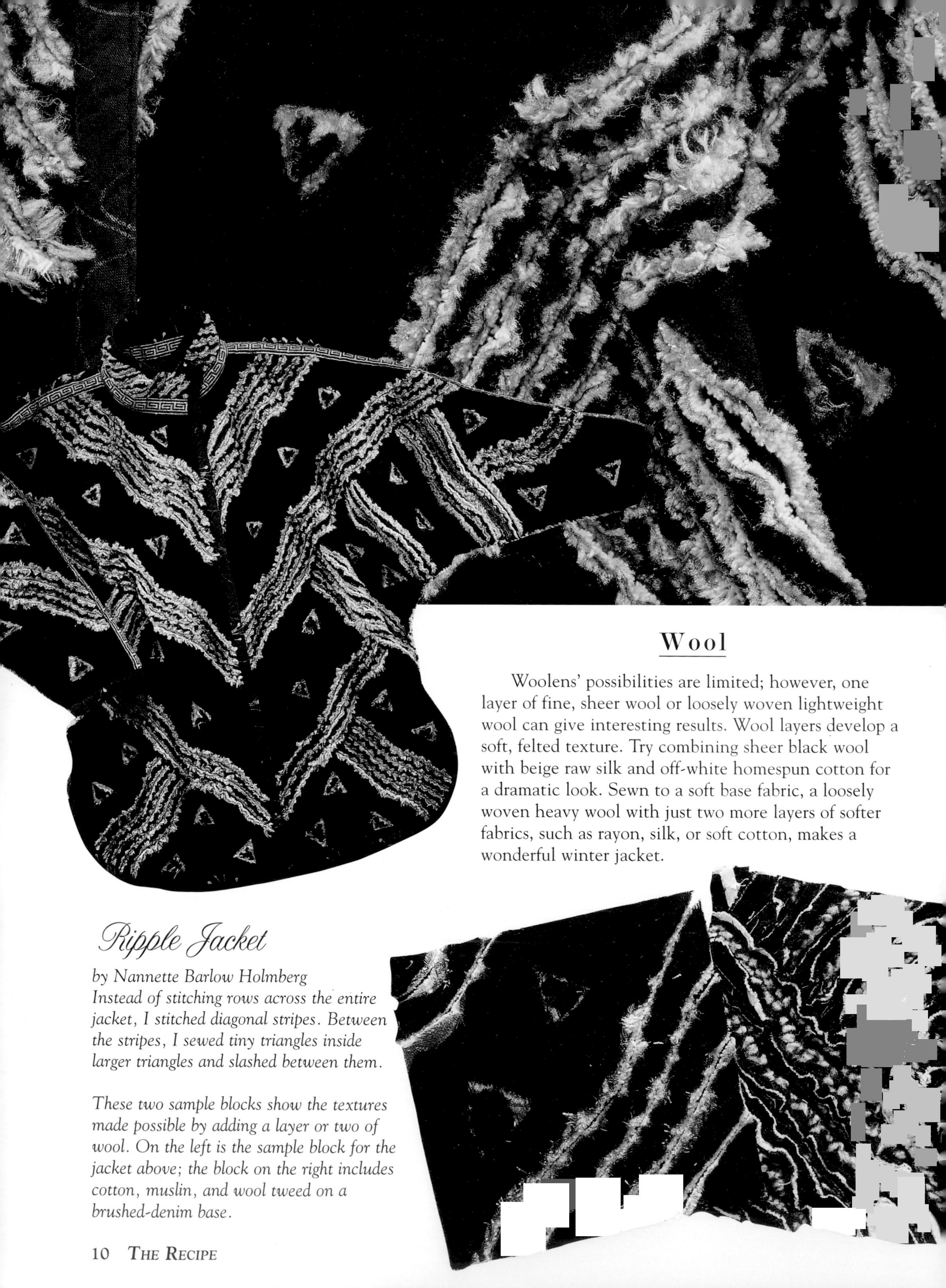

Wool

Woolens' possibilities are limited; however, one layer of fine, sheer wool or loosely woven lightweight wool can give interesting results. Wool layers develop a soft, felted texture. Try combining sheer black wool with beige raw silk and off-white homespun cotton for a dramatic look. Sewn to a soft base fabric, a loosely woven heavy wool with just two more layers of softer fabrics, such as rayon, silk, or soft cotton, makes a wonderful winter jacket.

Ripple Jacket

by Nannette Barlow Holmberg
Instead of stitching rows across the entire jacket, I stitched diagonal stripes. Between the stripes, I sewed tiny triangles inside larger triangles and slashed between them.

These two sample blocks show the textures made possible by adding a layer or two of wool. On the left is the sample block for the jacket above; the block on the right includes cotton, muslin, and wool tweed on a brushed-denim base.

Cotton

Cotton is a remarkable fabric. It lends itself to just about every wearable-art technique. It makes the transition from the two-dimensional world of quilting to the three-dimensional world of wearable art with ease.

But wait! As you roam through your favorite quilt shop looking for fabric to turn into chenille, remember a few things. You're not selecting fabric for a quilt, so don't pull out the wonderful prints and coordinated country cottons that you used in your favorite quilting project. These beautiful blended combinations and subtle colorations will be lost in chenille. Fasten your seat belt and let your inhibitions fly. Begin by looking just for color. Select fabrics with large, dramatic prints and hues, with a variety of color changes. Don't be afraid to mix a purple print with a chartreuse print and then add a navy blue solid and a few other solids. Think in terms of mixing a palette. These colors and prints will blend to create a new coloration. If you like the colors but hate the print, you've probably made a good choice.

Choose cotton prints in which the dye saturates the wrong side of the fabric. If a fabric looks richly colored on the right side but pale and washed out on the wrong side, it may not provide the color you want after it has been washed. A fabric with weak dye saturation can give a garment an old, frayed appearance. Of course, this may be just the look you want. Experiment!

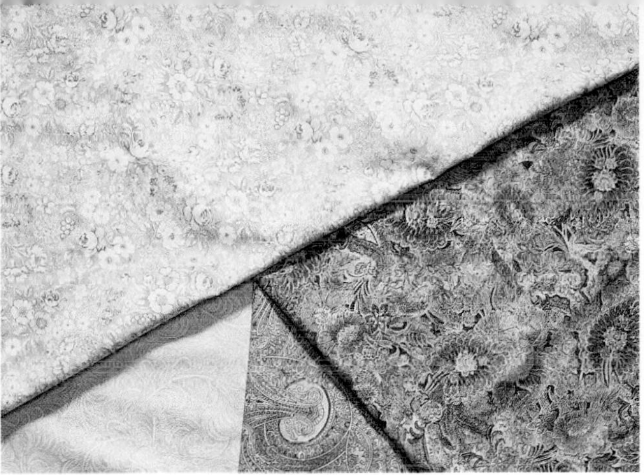

These fabrics don't show enough variation in color and value to make dramatic chenille.

Including one or two layers of fabric with strong, contrasting colors and values adds life to chenille.

The wrong sides of these cotton prints don't have enough dye to show good color when they bloom.

The wrong sides of these fabrics show good dye saturation.

Avoid cottons that feel stiff or coated on the right side, even if they are marked 100% cotton. This stiffness can prevent the fabric from blooming when it is washed and dried. When stiff fabric is used in the top layers, the garment may not bloom at all. If you have a questionable fabric, be sure to test it first by making sample blocks. (See "Sample Blocks" on page 25.)

These blocks—made from treated cottons—didn't bloom at all after they were washed.

Laura Munson Reinstatler made this chenille jacket from inexpensive cottons that she found on the flat-fold table. While they felt a little stiff, Laura assumed the finish would disappear after washing. The blocks on the facing page show the disappointing results of the first samples. Wanting a dark fabric on top, Laura substituted a soft cotton for layer #1. The result, while not a luxurious chenille, is intriguing and beautiful.

The cottons you choose don't need to have the same finish or texture; in fact, chenille works better when there are several different textures or weave structures. Loosely woven cottons, such as cotton gauze and homespun, work well every time, adding texture and depth to layers of closely woven cotton. Vary your fabric combinations in every way possible.

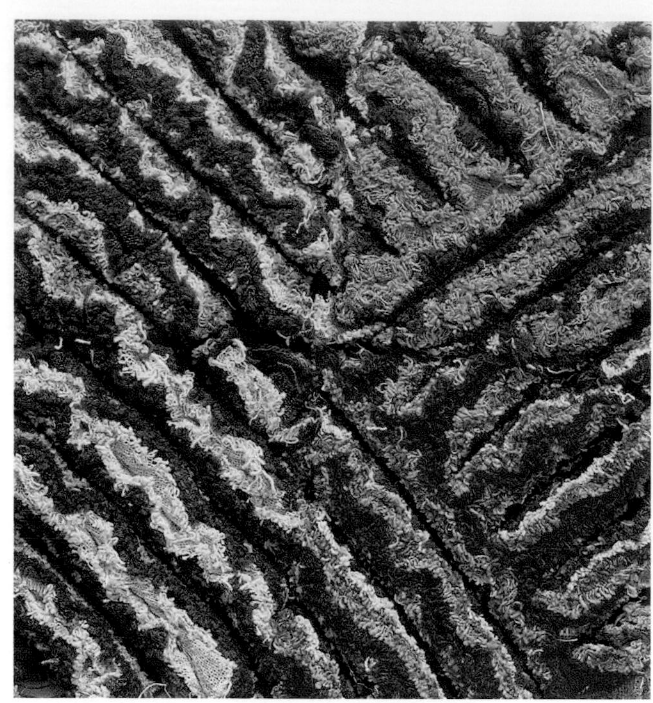

The sample shown below left is made of several layers of cotton gauze and one layer of cotton batting. The other samples, both sewn to a denim base, include cottons, rayons, and cotton denims.

The sample shown at right is made of different-colored layers of cotton gauze.

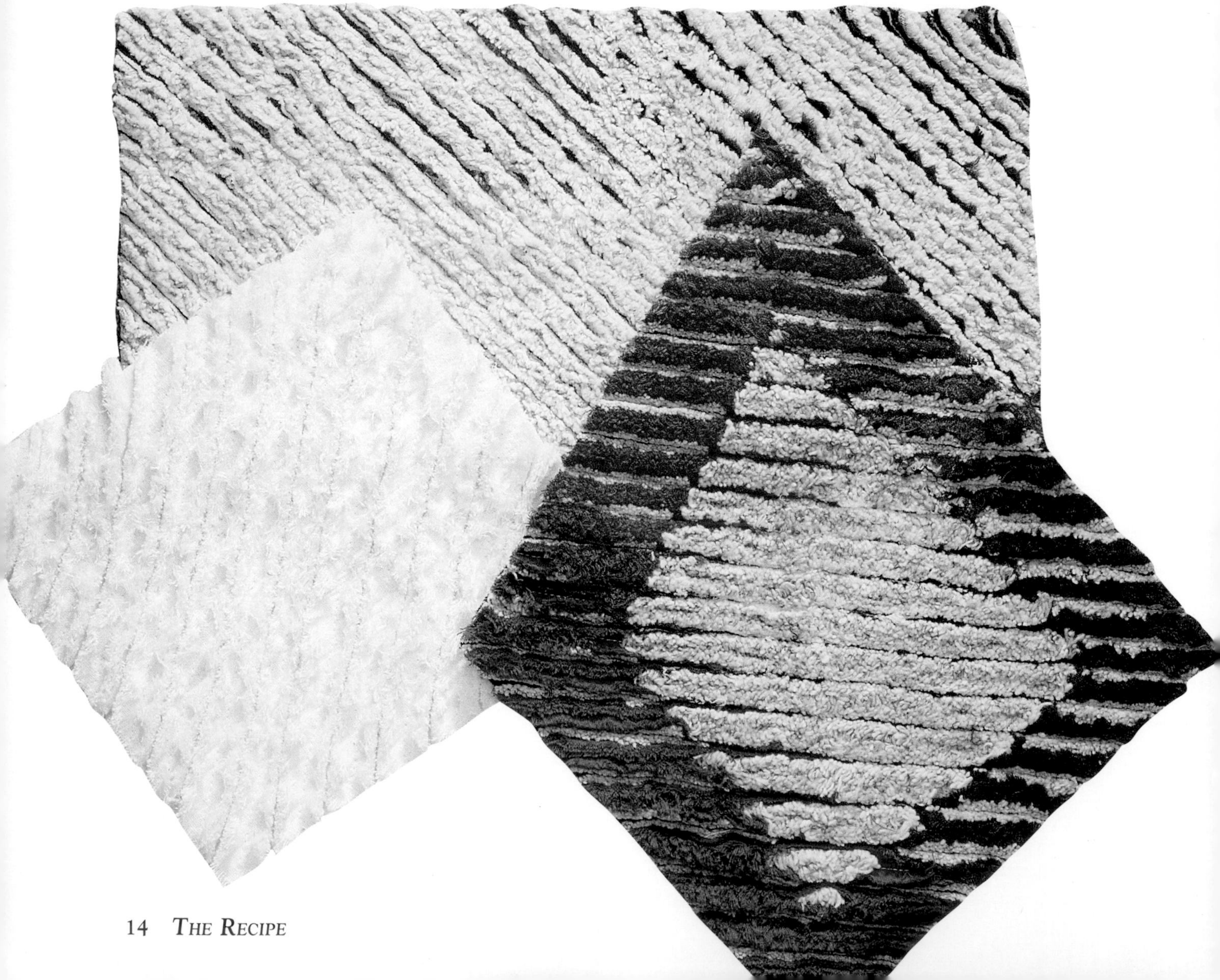

If you purchase fabrics for your project instead of using fabric from your stash, don't immediately buy yardage of the fabrics you select. Pull out bolts of several possibilities and color combinations, and buy only six inches of each fabric (or more, depending on the minimum amount of fabric the shop allows).

Go home and make sample blocks as described on pages 25–33. You'll be glad you did. Combine your new fabrics with a few pieces from your stash. If your combinations are wonderful, you can return the next day and buy the yardage for your jacket. If things don't work out, return to the store and look for something totally different.

Try combining cottons with other fabrics. One or two layers of cotton can add body to soft rayons and give depth to silks and woolens. Lightweight denims, soft damasks or jacquards, and muslin, as well as related fabrics such as linens and other flax-based fabrics, are good candidates.

Combining types of cotton fabric also works well. Cotton denim and cotton madras are perfect when used together for a casual look. If you're lucky, the madras colors will bleed and create an unexpected coloration.

This sample includes denim, rayon, and cotton madras plaid.

If you're having trouble making your cotton fabrics create a true chenille, or if your sample blocks have a rough texture you don't like, you can add a "secret ingredient."

A new product on the market is needlepunched 100% cotton batting that is soft, lightweight, and perfect for wearables. The only drawback is that needlepunched batting is currently produced only in white and off-white—although, because it is 100% cotton, it can be dyed. Using needlepunched batting as the bottom layer next to your base, then adding three or four layers of cotton prints, solids, and even muslin, allows you to change the flat look of washed cottons into luxurious chenille. If you decide to try batting as one of your layers, be sure to use 100% cotton, *needlepunched* batting. I've had success with Warm & Natural by The Warm Company and Soft Touch by Fairfield Processing Corporation.

Needlepunched cotton batting

Cotton battings that are not needlepunched

You must realize, however, that although needlepunched batting will give your cottons the look of chenille, your chenille will have a different hand and drape than if you were to use rayons, silks, or other fibers. Most cottons have more body than rayons and some types of silk; therefore, chenille that includes cotton batting will have more body and less drape. Adding a layer of needlepunched batting brings other cotton layers to life; many cottons that otherwise would appear flat and lifeless bloom and create elegant chenille in the company of batting. And remember, you can dye needlepunched batting to use with dark fabrics. Try this "secret ingredient" if you're ever disappointed with cottons. For more ideas, see "Secret Ingredients" on page 21.

This early sample for the jacket shown on the facing page is layered with cotton fabrics only. The combination lacks the depth and richness of the samples made with a layer of batting.

While this sample blooms more successfully than the first sample, the batting layer next to the base fabric creates a sharp visual contrast. The rows stand out individually instead of working together in an even texture.

This is the sample block for the jacket, with batting as the fourth layer. The fabric in layer #5 provides a visual transition from the base fabric to the chenille layers, contributing to the even and luxurious overall effect.

Pink and Blue

by Nannette Barlow Holmberg
Layers of cotton prints and solids, when combined with a layer of needlepunched cotton batting, combine for a rich, luxurious appearance. The variations in print, color, and value contribute to the visual interest.

Try needlepunched cotton batting with rayons and other fabric combinations. Although the garment is technically quilted with a layer of batting, you don't get the heavy, cumbersome look of so many quilted garments. The batting drapes because it has been cut in rows. This slashing allows the garment to maintain the soft draping qualities of the base (uncut) layer of fabric.

Velvet Autumn

by Nannette Barlow Holmberg
Layers of cotton batting and muslin, and synthetic suede trim, make this jacket practical yet elegant. A great casual look with denim for running errands, it also works beautifully with silk noil for evenings on the town. Synthetic suede leaf appliqués accent the unslashed "windowpanes" on the jacket back.

Rayon

Rayon is perhaps my greatest chenille discovery. For optimum results, use 100% rayons, although rayons blended with other natural fibers such as cotton, linen, or silk offer possibilities. Rayon-polyester blends won't bloom. Your sample blocks will indicate which fabrics to use.

Rayon challis is the best staple for chenille. Because it is soft and drapable, it will maintain a soft hand and lightweight appearance in a completed jacket. Its soft drape also adds less bulk to the silhouette. Rayon is available in a nice range of solid colors that are a great addition when worked into other fabric combinations.

Rayon prints are often bold and dramatic. The flat-fold or clearance table frequently offers the wildest and most obnoxious rayon prints—look at the stunning example on page 7 and the jacket on page 8. Don't be afraid to choose a large-scale, boisterous print for the top or next-to-top layer of your chenille stack. Bold prints are perfect for this layer, where the colorations will be most apparent. The samples shown here illustrate how effective this type of print can be. Keep in mind that these fabrics will be stitched together and slashed—the final product will be a blend of colors rather than a distinct pattern.

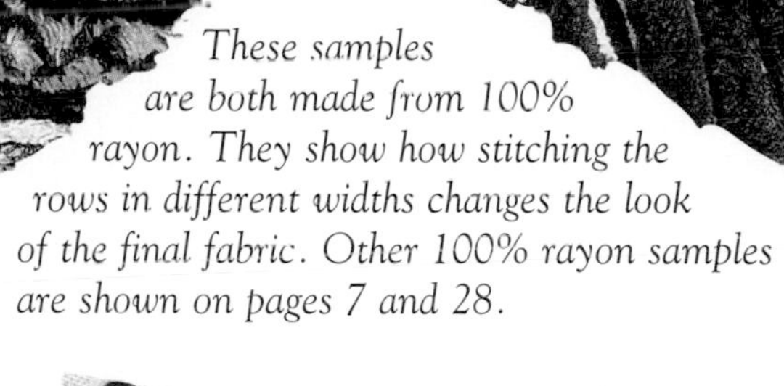

These samples are both made from 100% rayon. They show how stitching the rows in different widths changes the look of the final fabric. Other 100% rayon samples are shown on pages 7 and 28.

These bold and dramatic rayon prints would make wonderful additions to a chenille stack.

This sample block is made from black shibori-discharged rayon layers combined with one solid black layer. The patterning of the shibori layers creates wonderful lines and colorations.

Rayon comes in a variety of weaves, weights, and textures. Don't limit yourself to the soft rayon challis prints and solids. Rayon crepes and crinkled rayons are wonderful and provide great texture, as do the mesh fabrics so popular now in sportswear.

In general, all types of 100% rayon are effective except those that have been put through a stone- or sandwashing process. This process changes the fiber, causing it to act like polyester. Stonewashed fabrics in general, and silks and rayons especially, will not be successful in chenille projects except for use as the lining or base layer.

Jewels

Layer #2 of this jacket is the bold, geometric print shown below. The sharp edges of the print are softened by the layers of chenille. Garment designed and fabrics selected by Nannette Barlow Holmberg. Made by Laura Munson Reinstatler from McCall's pattern 8528.

Fabrics that Don't Work

Synthetic fibers, such as polyesters and acetates, will fail all chenille tests. A rayon- or cotton-polyester blend—if placed on top of other fibers—will lie lifeless, keeping other workable fabrics from doing their thing. It doesn't matter how wonderful the color or how incredible the print, if it has polyester in it, don't use it as a chenille layer. (You can, however, use some of these fabrics for the base layer. See page 24.)

Fabrics with pile or nap, such as velvet, corduroy, and velour, are generally too bulky and don't need to be considered here. Some cotton velveteens, however, work fairly well when layered with other, softer fabrics, such as rayons.

It is possible to cheat a little. For example, if the fabric in question is a piece that you feel you must use for color and it doesn't want to cooperate in your sample blocks, layer it next to the base. Or, you might place it as the second layer from the base and let the layers above it bloom.

Secret Ingredients

To energize a flat sample of chenille, try adding one or more layers of the following fabrics to your stack. As you add fabrics, remove the same number of unsuccessful fabric squares.

A loosely woven fabric such as a rayon mesh or cotton homespun will always add texture and loft to a stack. One or more layers of gauze will also give chenille a wonderful texture. Gauze is available in a wide range of colors, or you can dye white or natural-colored gauze the desired color.

Needlepunched cotton batting will bring a stack of cottons to life, but it should be placed next to the base fabric or in the layer #4 position. (See the samples on pages 16–17.)

In general, the addition of loosely woven fabrics such as silks and fine woolens produces a beautiful loft and soft texture.

Chenille comes alive when several secret ingredients, such as batting and gold lamé, are combined.

Novelty Fabrics and Trims

Consider using novelty fabrics, such as tissue lamé and rayon-embroidered laces. Tissue lamé adds glamour and takes chenille from daytime to evening. Bridal-lace yardage embroidered with shiny satin thread jazzes up a stack of muslin and cotton jacquard. Although all these fabrics are labeled "dry clean only," you will find that many of them launder just fine in a chenille stack. But don't use tricot lamé for this technique. Tricot lamé has a knit backing, so instead of fraying, the tricot backing curls when washed, which won't enhance the chenille. It won't fare well in the dryer either. Tissue lamé, because it is woven, blooms beautifully.

Hand-dyed layers of rayon and cotton batting

This sample block's chenille layers, sewn to a muslin background, include cotton jacquard and rayon lace.

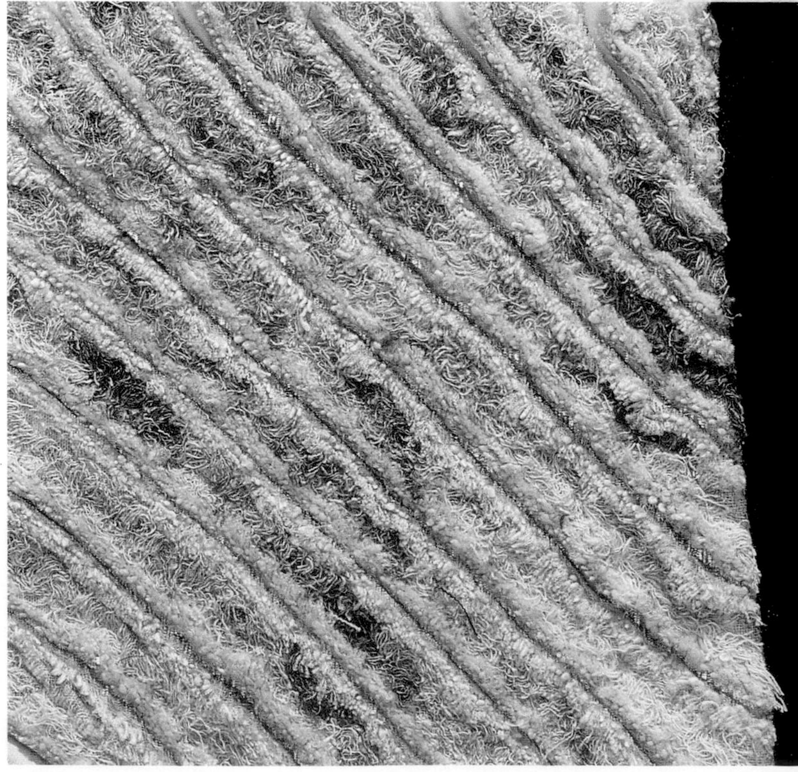

Black velvet ribbon makes an elegant trim or binding.

Don't be afraid to try new products on the market, regardless of their washing or dry-cleaning directions. Just be sure to test them first. Make a sample block of selected fabrics and apply the ribbon or trim in the same manner that you would apply it to the garment. For example, if you want to use ribbon as binding, stitch the ribbon to the edge of the block. If it will be a trim, apply it as you would to the surface of the garment.

Grosgrain ribbons, metallic braids, and silk-embroidered ribbons all work well on chenille garments and go through washing and drying beautifully. You may decide to bind a jacket with rich black velvet for extra elegance. I have used bias-cut velvet fabric for binding and trim, and black velvet ribbon for trim. (See the sample block on the facing page.)

Rarely when discussing fabrics do I use the words "always" or "never." It is generally a process of exploration and elimination. Choosing fabrics and creating sample blocks for your finished process should be fun and filled with unexpected results. The most luscious chenille will be the result of time, patience, and experimentation. Make your recipe and your journey a personal one and, like a family recipe, one worth keeping!

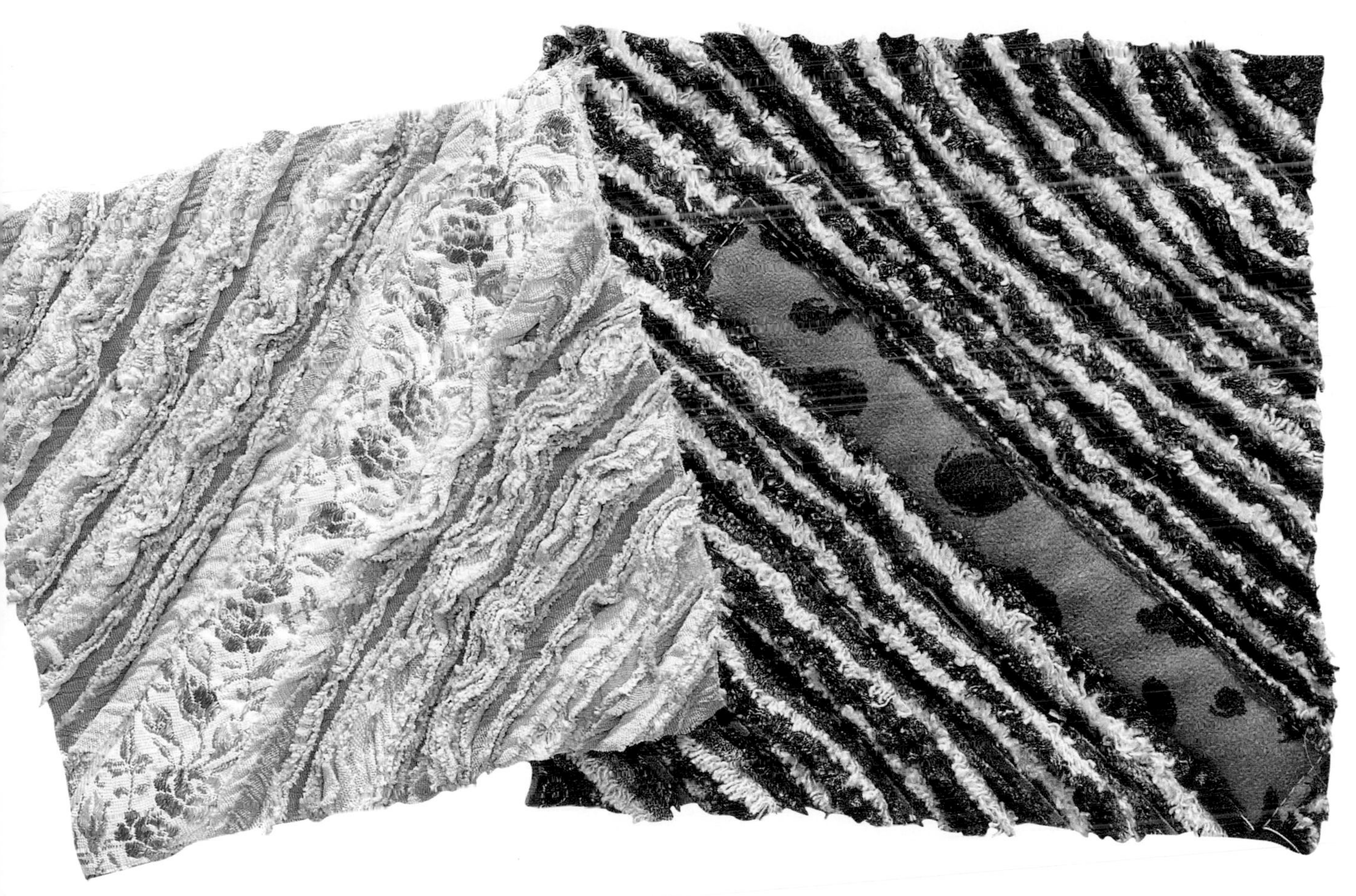

The Base Layer

When it comes to the base layer, you have more options than for the chenille layers. The base layer remains intact. It won't be slashed and doesn't need to bloom. Because of this you can experiment.

The base layer becomes the lining of the jacket or vest. Some of the fabrics on the Do-Not-Use list are suddenly okay when considered for the base. Try satins and even polyesters. Select a fabric that you like and want to see intact when you open your jacket. It may be a solid color that coordinates with the colors in your chenille, or you may prefer a stripe or print—small or bold—that gives the lining a designer touch. Be sure to choose a fabric that looks good on both sides. Keep in mind that a small amount of this layer will show on the outside of the garment, between the rows of chenille.

The hand-dyed base layer of this sample square shows between the layers of chenille.

The hand-dyed base fabric for the sample shown at left

Sample Blocks

Making sample blocks is the part I enjoy most. Sample blocks are critical to the success of the finished project. Creating a successful sample before you begin the project means that all the work you put into the finished article will be worthwhile. Failing to make samples could set you up for a huge disappointment when your finished piece comes out of the dryer.

Creating sample blocks before beginning a chenille project is an exciting process in itself. Chenille's finished look is always unexpected, and it would be unfortunate to miss the fun of experiencing each new piece. When different fibers, colors, and textures are combined in a stack and put through the process of washing and drying, there will be a total metamorphosis; the colorations you create will be a surprise.

Take the time to explore possibilities. When experimenting, don't limit yourself to only five or six fabrics; you'll have better success with a good assortment of fibers, colors, and textures.

When making chenille, I usually like to work with six layers of fabric. Because each fabric is different, I get six different results when I layer each stack in a different order. In most cases, only one or two combinations make a nice chenille even though each stack has identical fabrics.

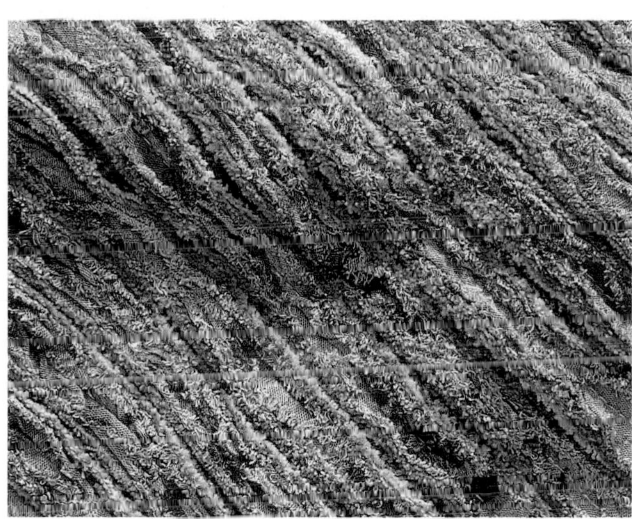

The fabrics in this sample block are identical to the fabrics in the blocks below. A change in fabric order can make a dramatic difference.

When compared to the successful combination of fabrics above, these blocks are clearly unsatisfactory.

Both of these sample blocks show two trial arrangements on one square. For each block, I cut two stacks of triangles, layered them differently, stitched the rows in different directions on a square of base fabric, then laundered the blocks. For "The Captain in Chenille" (page 50), I selected the layering arrangement in the upper right corner of the block on the right. Can you see the difference in the chenille effects?

After assembling a variety of fabrics from your private stash and the fabric store, you are ready to make sample blocks. (Remember, *do not* prewash the fabrics before beginning the chenille process.)

Combinations of some fabrics will not work at all. The results may be completely flat. If all your layering combinations fail but you really want to use the fabrics, try adding one or more of the secret ingredients described on page 21. They always bring successful results.

Be aware of colors in your stack and what they can do. Many colors can dominate and overpower other fabrics. Colors create different effects when layered on the table than when they bloom after washing. Red and other vibrant colors such as orange or purple will dominate and sometimes overpower otherwise wonderful combinations.

Dramatic fabrics create striped effects when used as the top layer. Black or navy on top of a fabric stack will create a subtle stripe in the chenille's pattern. The higher red and other bright colors are placed in the layered stack, the more they will stand out.

You will save time in the long run by constructing, washing, and drying all the sample-square combinations at one time instead of making them one by one. Seeing all the blocks at once as they come out of the dryer allows you to make immediate comparisons. Making the blocks individually may mean a lot of waiting, only to discover you need to try another combination of squares and wait some more.

To make a sample block, cut 6" x 6" squares from each of the selected fabrics. (I usually cut six squares from each fabric.) Stack the squares according to fabric, then line up the stacks across the back of a table.

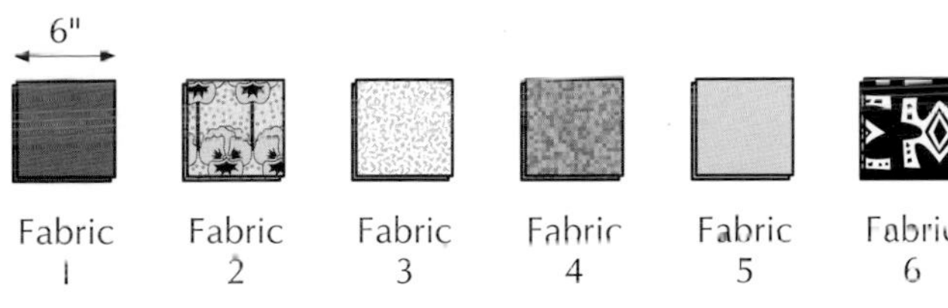

Begin stacking squares, placing each fabric square in a different order in each stack. Place the first square on the bottom of the first stack (it will be the base layer), place it second in the second stack, third in the third stack, and so on. If you layer your stacks systematically, you'll avoid confusion and get better results.

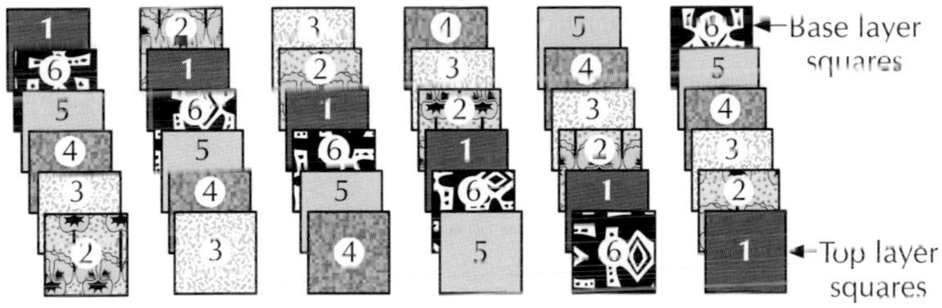

Base layer squares

Top layer squares

Note: Two layers of the same fabric may work better than one layer of each fabric from your stacks. Keep repeat fabric layers in mind.

Don't decide ahead of time that you want a specific square on top. You may find that your chosen fabric doesn't work at all the way you thought it would. The photo below shows an excellent example of predetermined layers that didn't work out. In this case, I wanted the printed fabric to be the top layer. I made six stacks, with each stack layered in a different order, except the top layer. I used the print for each top layer because I was certain I wanted the colorations of the print to dominate the colors in the chenille. I was after the wonderful effect that I found in the jacket shown on page 8.

After I stitched, cut, washed, and dried all six stacks, I was disappointed. Each block was flat and undesirable for use in a finished project.

These sample squares refused to bloom, despite my desire to use the print for the top layer!

Although I was sure this fabric combination was just not going to work, I decided to give it one more try since I had spent so much time on it already. I moved the print down several layers and moved a few of the solids to the top. The result was the chenille fabric you see in this jacket.

This garment taught me to have an open mind about layer combinations. Predetermining the order of fabrics may cause you to overlook wonderful possibilities.

Lavender Sachet

by Nannette Barlow Holmberg
At first, I wanted the print in this jacket to be the top layer. When the sample blocks showed it wouldn't work, I changed its position in the stack, with successful results.

Compare this sample with the unsuccessful ones shown on page 27. Moving the print gave the chenille a dramatically different look.

The base layer is the only layer that you can safely choose ahead of time because it won't be cut and will not effect the final fluff of the chenille. It is interesting, however, to see the top cut layers of chenille against a variety of lining or base colors. Again, the results may surprise you.

Once you've layered all your stacks you can begin stitching.

1. Place the base fabric *right side down*, then layer the remaining fabric squares on top, *right side up*. Pin the sample stack in a few places to keep it straight and easy to work with.

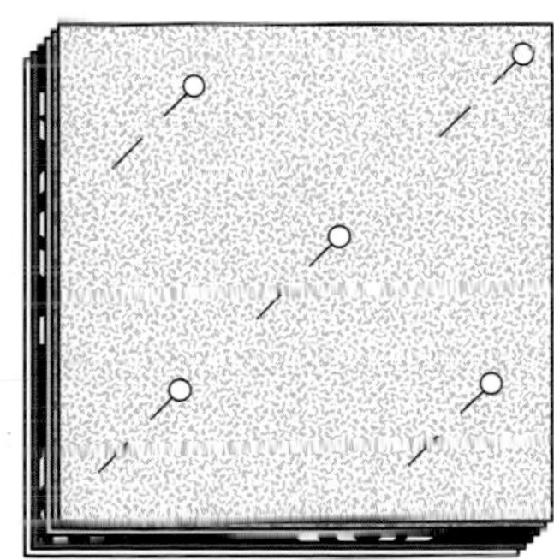

2. Using a ruler for accuracy, draw a line from corner to corner on the right side of the top layer. Move the pins if they are in the way of the ruler.

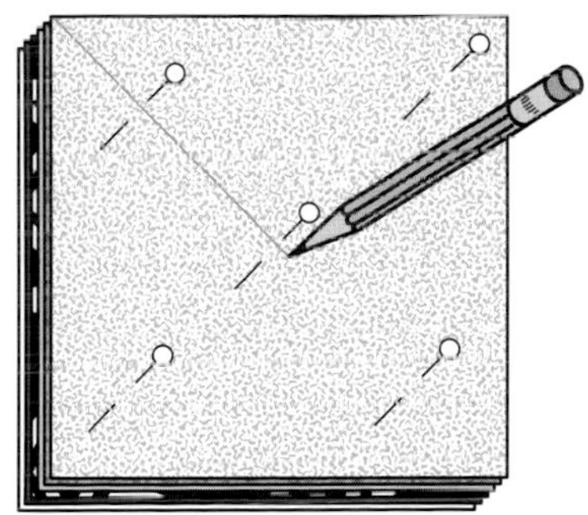

Tip

To make the stitching rows easier to see, select a color for the top thread that contrasts slightly with the fabric. For example, if the top layer is black, use a gray or navy thread in the needle. The stitching will be hidden after you wash your jacket.

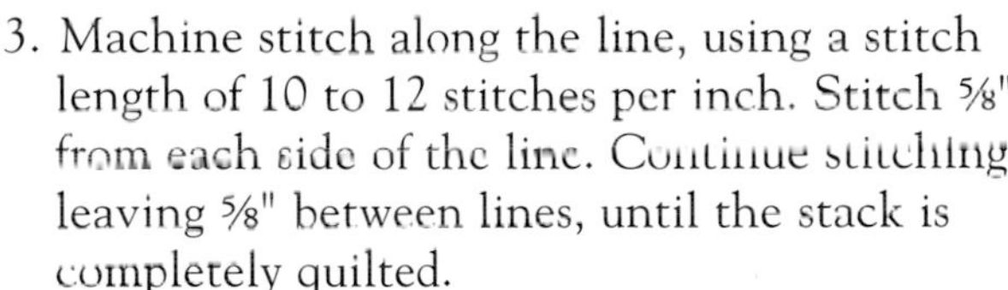

3. Machine stitch along the line, using a stitch length of 10 to 12 stitches per inch. Stitch ⅝" from each side of the line. Continue stitching, leaving ⅝" between lines, until the stack is completely quilted.

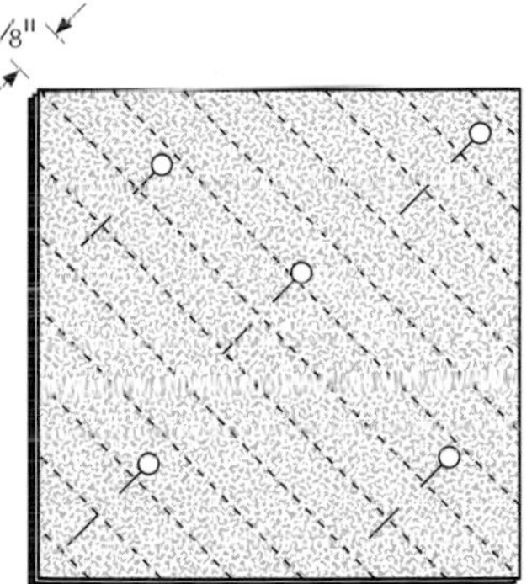

4. Cut the top 5 layers between the stitching lines. Take care not to cut the bottom layer, or base, which must remain intact.

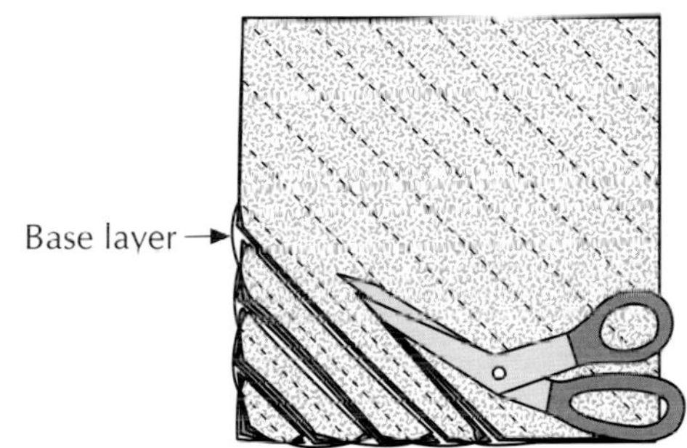

Choosing Your Stitch

Angles

To create the softest, richest, most consistent chenille, stitch the rows at a 45° angle to the straight grain of the fabric. If you like the effect a different angle gives—great! Just be sure to be consistent throughout your project. If you begin by stitching rows at a 45° angle, don't let the angle gradually change.

An advantage of selecting a 45° angle is that the threads that make up the fabric are held uniformly by the stitches. When slashed and laundered, the fabric frays and fluffs evenly on both sides of the stitching. The closer the angle of stitching approaches the straight of grain (either lengthwise or crosswise), the more shredding or stringing you get. In the sample shown below, notice how the 30°-angle stitching at left looks much shaggier than the other stitching. The long strings make the chenille floppy, and it may even be necessary to give the chenille a "haircut" to make it look presentable.

You can create striking effects by alternating the direction of the stitched rows. Laura Munson Reinstatler's "Wine Cooler" jacket, shown on page 43, illustrates how stitching variations add interest to the overall design. Peggy Neeley's "Mikado" jacket, shown on page 44, is another example of the drama made possible by changing the stitching direction. If you decide to vary the direction of your stitching rows, remember to stitch at an angle to the grain line.

The zigzag stitching pattern creates marvelous texture in these layers of shibori-discharged black rayon.

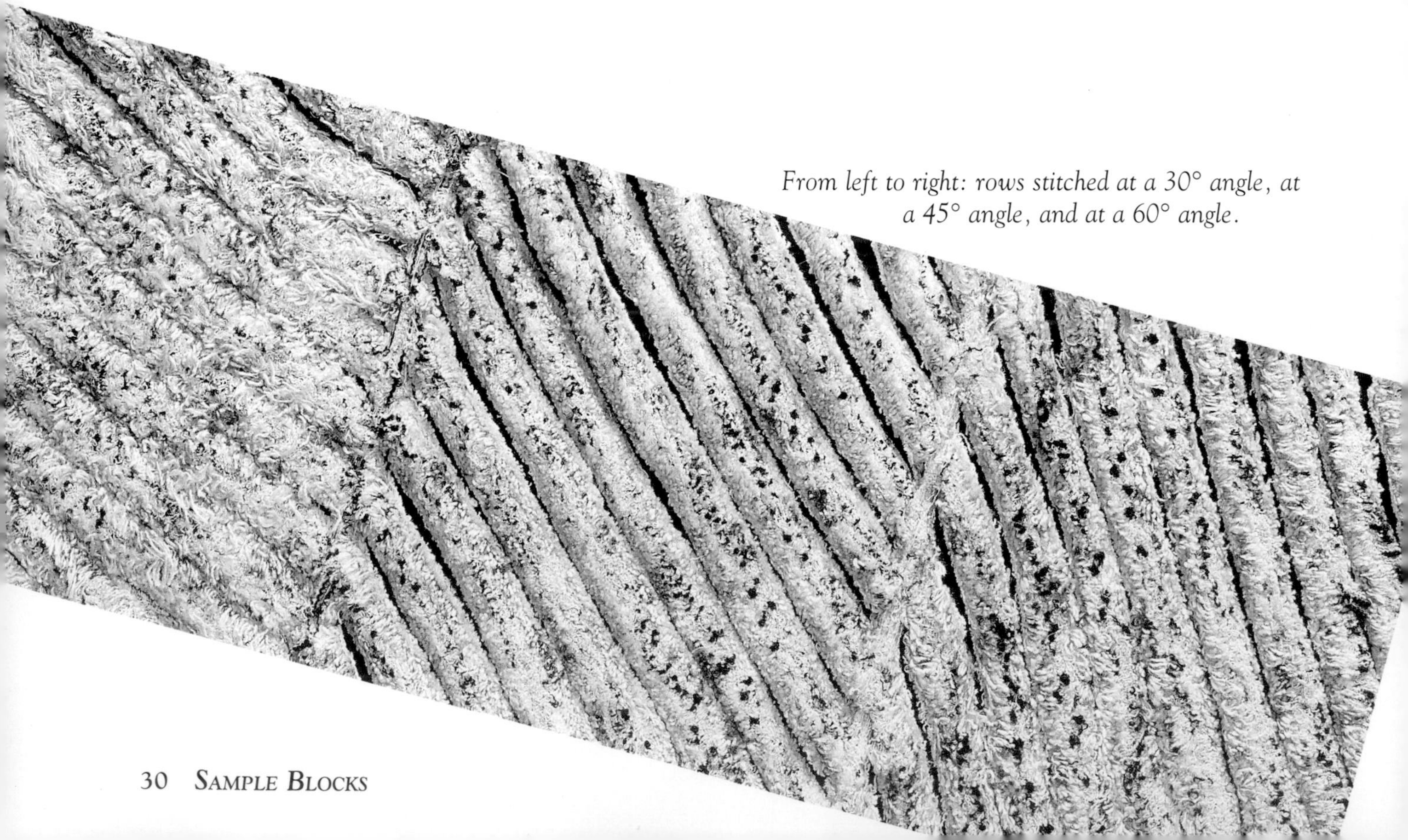

From left to right: rows stitched at a 30° angle, at a 45° angle, and at a 60° angle.

Width between Rows

Stitching the rows ⅝" apart gives me a soft chenille with the look of the old-fashioned chenille for which I named it. Experiment with rows of different widths. If you leave less than ½" between rows, you may lose the chenille's rich texture, because there's not much fabric to fray and fluff up between rows.

Stitching rows farther apart than ⅝" sometimes creates floppy chenille and shows more of the lining. Widely spaced rows can be very effective when worked in loosely woven fabrics and can create almost a fringed effect.

When I want to experiment with different widths between rows, I usually stitch half the block in one width and the other half in another width. Then I can compare the effects without having to make extra blocks.

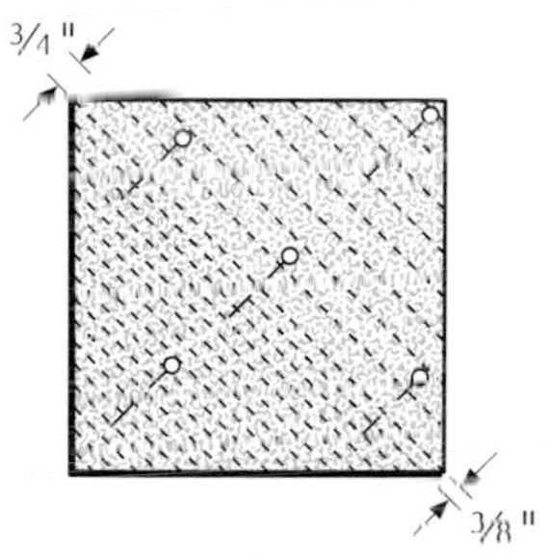

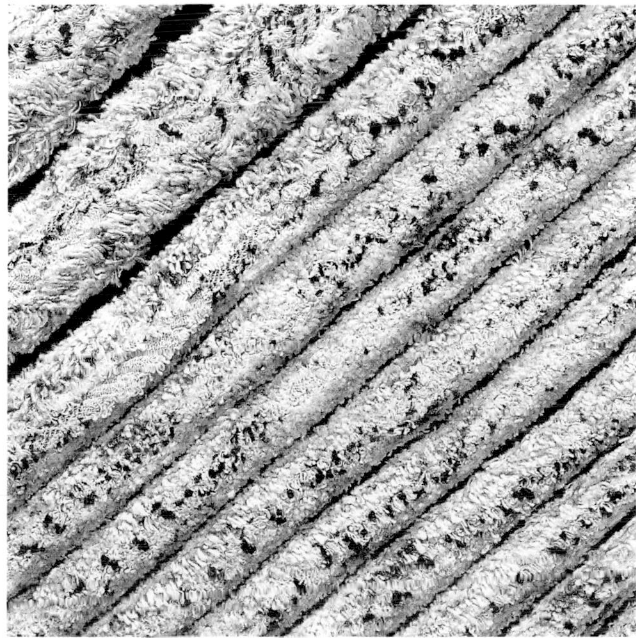

By varying the distance between stitching rows, you can achieve dramatically different effects. The rows at the lower right are ½" to ⅝" apart, while the rows at upper left are 1" to 1¼" apart.

Mending Cuts and Holes

Even when you use blunt-nosed scissors and pay careful attention to your work, accidents can occur when you slash your project. A hole may appear in the middle of your jacket, or you might accidentally cut an edge a few inches before realizing what you've done. Your first reaction will be to panic, but all your hard work can be saved.

First, measure the length of the opening. Cut a rectangle of base fabric 1" longer than the hole and 2½" wide. Cut a piece of fusible webbing the same size as the patch.

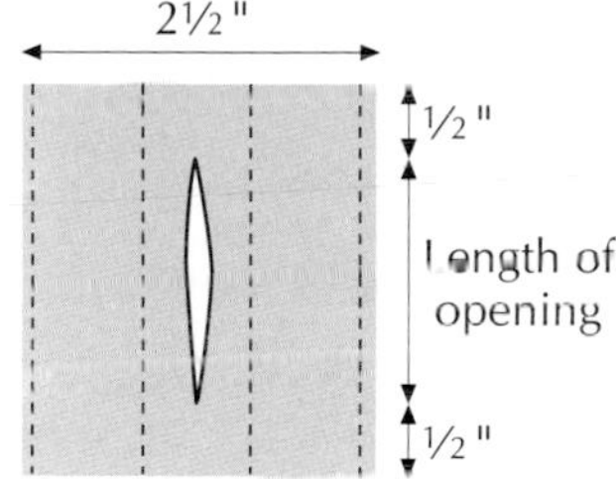

Following the manufacturer's directions, apply fusible web to the wrong side of the patch. When cool, peel off the paper and place the patch over the hole, on the inside (backing fabric) of your project. Center the patch ½" beyond each end of the cut and 1¼" to each side. Press to fuse.

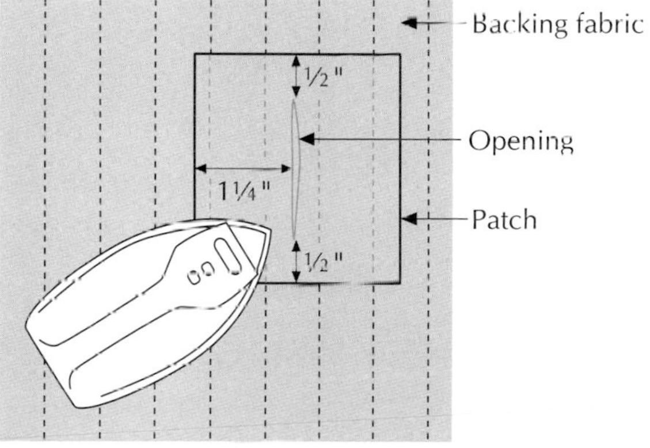

Turn the project right (slashed) side up. To reinforce the mending, sew on top of the lines you just stitched.

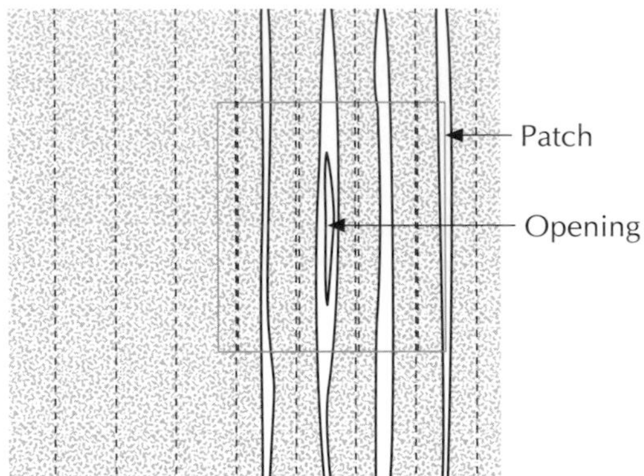

Note: If the mending piece is in a visible spot inside your garment, turn your mistake into a design detail by covering the hole with a cut-out floral print or geometric shape. Fuse a few more flowers or shapes inside your jacket. Now you have designer details. Suddenly you're thrilled that the mistake happened!

This patch is difficult to see because it blends so well with the backing fabric.

This flower patch is so well integrated, it's hard to believe it's not printed on the fabric.

Laundering Chenille

After you've cut all your stacks, they're ready to go through the laundering process.

1. At a sink, wet the blocks and wring them out. Hand agitate each block by rubbing it against itself until you see the rows begin to fluff up and separate from the base fabric. If your fabrics don't fluff—no matter how much you scrub the block—there's a good chance the chenille won't come up in the dryer either.

Agitating the block

Fluffed and separated rows

This block, no matter how much it is tormented, refuses to fluff or separate.

Note: *After wetting and agitating each block, you will find a huge mess of thread and lint in your sink. The same thing will happen in your dryer, so be sure your lint filter is clean before you dry the blocks.*

2. Place the blocks in the dryer with a few old towels. Set the dryer at a medium setting, then check the blocks after 15 minutes. Don't remove them until they are completely dry.

When the blocks go into the dryer, only the top layer of the stack shows, and the look of the block is rough. When you come back to the dryer in fifteen minutes or so (and if your fabrics have bloomed correctly), you'll be amazed at the metamorphosis that has taken place. You'll find yourself waiting anxiously by the dryer, as I do, to see the final results.

Laundering large pieces, such as garments or wall hangings, is similar to the process for the sample blocks. Place the garment in the washing machine by itself. Do not wash it for the first time with other things because there will be a great deal of lint (more for some fabrics than for others). This lint will make a mess on the other items. Set the machine for a short cycle, regular or delicate, with a warm wash and cold rinse. I add about one tablespoon of detergent, but it's not necessary. I do it to remove any finish the fabrics might have.

Dry the piece by itself in the dryer at a medium setting. Be sure the lint filter is empty when you put your garment in the dryer. It's a good idea to check the lint filter during the drying time too. The garment must be completely dry before you remove it from the dryer.

Clean the lint filter again after you remove the piece from the dryer.

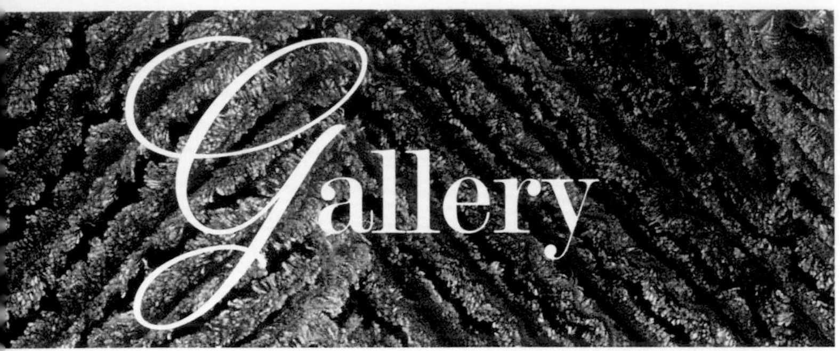

Gallery

Wearables are being recognized as art by collectors and gallery owners everywhere. Galleries and prestigious exhibitions throughout the United States show wearable art more and more. Many pieces are exhibited in collectors' homes and are purchased for preservation in museums' permanent collections.

As with any art form, wearable art reflects the soul of the artist—each approaches a technique in a personal way. The use of colors and fabrics in each piece represents individual visions.

The projects in this book offer "recipes" to start you on your artistic journey. The following section provides a glimpse of what is possible when artists use the recipes as pathways for innovation and expression. I hope that by making a chenille project and seeing how several artists have interpreted this technique, you'll be inspired to move beyond what you ever dreamed you could do.

Denim Friendly

by Nannette Barlow Holmberg
Recycled denim provides textural contrast while coordinating with the chenille coloration.

Tundra

by Kathleen Deneris
Kathleen chose a random pattern for the design. The resulting "furrows" provide a texture and pile that is fun to explore. Warm & Natural batting creates a unique surface texture and adds warmth, while muslin contributes a soft hand, making the layers easy to cut.

Winter Furrows

by Kathleen Deneris
Kathleen likes dyeing fabrics to make each piece a unique, creative statement. For this garment, she wanted to explore the potential of fiber-reactive dyes and selected Warm & Natural batting because it takes dye well. She stitched and slashed the pieces, then washed them several times to remove excess dye. Because of the way the fabrics took the dyes, the finished garment has a variegated look.

Moroccan Waves

by Kathleen Deneris
Kathleen followed the geometric print for the stitching patterns of this piece. The layered fabrics include cottons and rayons.

Fabric Watercolor

by Christine Bramhall

This project was the result of experimentation with Faux Chenille. Christine wanted to see what would happen if she randomly layered different colors in various shapes while concentrating some colors in certain areas. The outcome is at once subtle yet distinctive—not achievable through any other technique.

It'll All Come Out in the Wash

by Nannette Barlow Holmberg
Six different chenille colorations made this ensemble a show-stopping entry in Fairfield Processing Corporation's 1996 Fashion Show. A basic black jumpsuit sets off the colorations in the matching vest.

Patchwork

by Christine Bramhall
Christine's goal with this piece was to create texture and interest by using the humblest of fabrics, mere muslin. The madras plaid bias strips create a framework and lend cohesiveness to the design. The alternating stitching directions and randomly slashed and unslashed areas create interest.

Painted Desert

by Nannette Barlow Holmberg
Conchas and suede strips add a Southwest touch to the desert-inspired colorations in this jacket.

Jungle Fever

by Nannette Barlow Holmberg

The large-scale checked fabric used in the jacket's outer layer makes a perfect coordinating trim.

Wine Cooler

by Laura Munson Reinstatler
Laura chose a herringbone pattern for the top of this jacket's front and back. Design and fabric selection by Nannette Barlow Holmberg. McCall's pattern 8528.

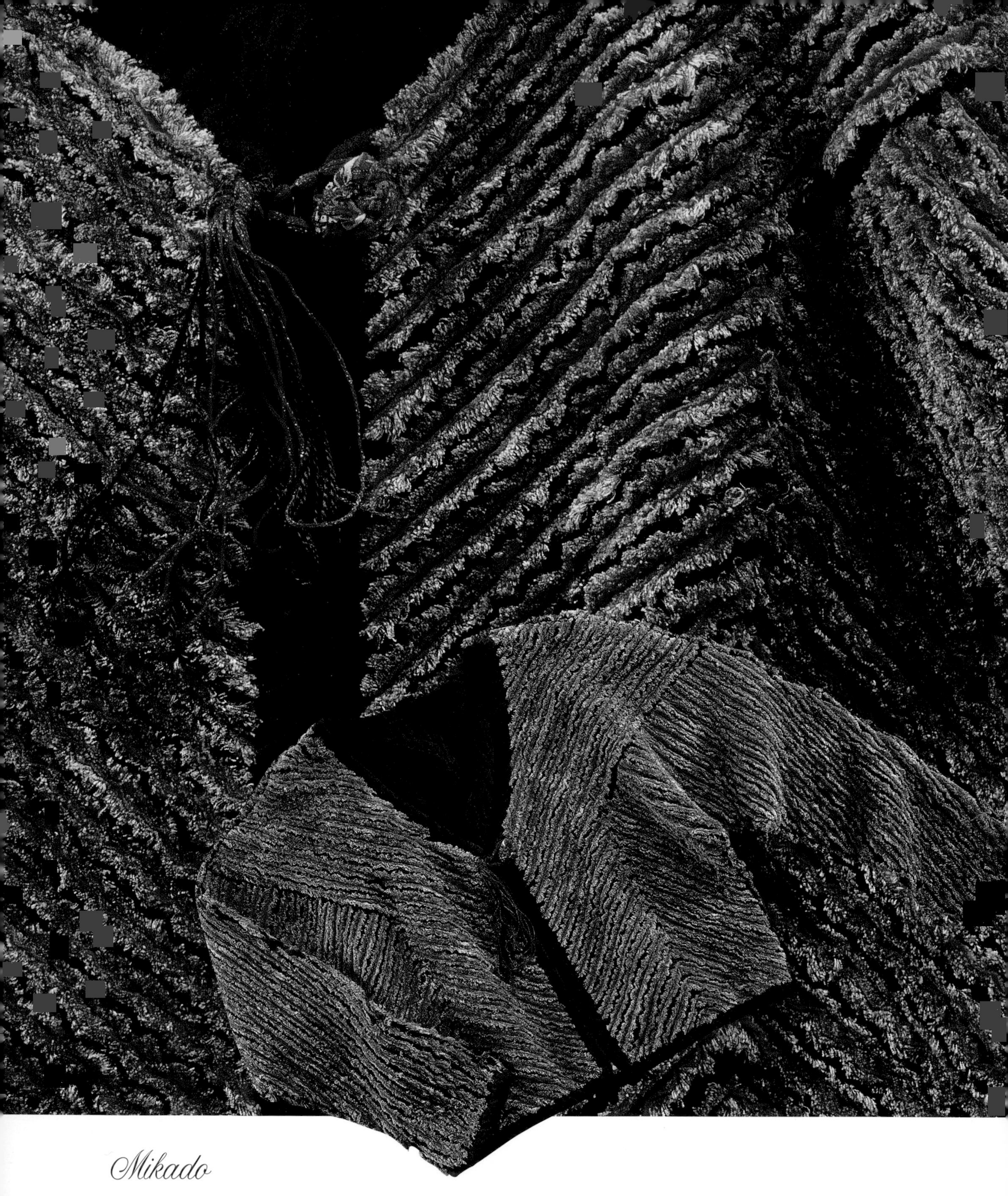

Mikado

by Peggy Neeley
Varied stitching directions enhance this beautiful coloration. The resulting pattern would flatter any body shape.

Untitled Jacket

by Nannette Barlow Holmberg
Teal-and-purple binding echoes the chenille's rich coloration.

Projects in Chenille

Note: For each of the projects, use ⅝"-wide seam allowances unless otherwise noted.

Selecting the Pattern

There are commercial patterns available that have been designed specifically for slashed chenille jackets and vests. Remember that slashed garments should be loose and larger than normal when you fit them—they will shrink when washed. The patterns in this book have been designed to accommodate the additional bulk created by the layered fabric and to allow for shrinkage.

If you want to use commercial patterns not designed for chenille, look for loose-fitting, unstructured styles. Dolman-, kimono-, and raglan-sleeve jackets can be adapted easily. The rule of thumb is to cut your jacket or vest two or more sizes larger than normal and add 1" to the sleeve and body lengths. It's wise to cut pattern pieces even larger and recut them to the final size after stitching and slashing.

Projects you want to try with the latticework technique—in which the base fabric doesn't shrink—can be made in a standard pattern size without alteration.

Note: The patterns in this book are larger than standard pattern sizes to allow for shrinkage. Choose the size you normally wear.

The size designations in this book correspond to the following dress sizes:

Pattern Size	Dress Size
Petite	4–6
Small	8–10
Medium	12–14
Large	16–18
Extra-large	20–22

Preparing the Pattern

The garment patterns on the following pages are drawn on grids. To make your pattern, draw a grid of 1" x 1" squares on a large piece of paper, such as blank newsprint.

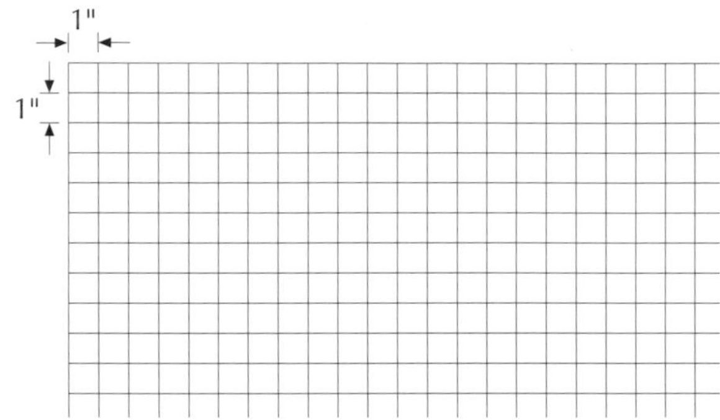

Transfer the pattern markings in the book to the corresponding square on your grid: 1 pattern square equals 1". Take care to copy the correct size.

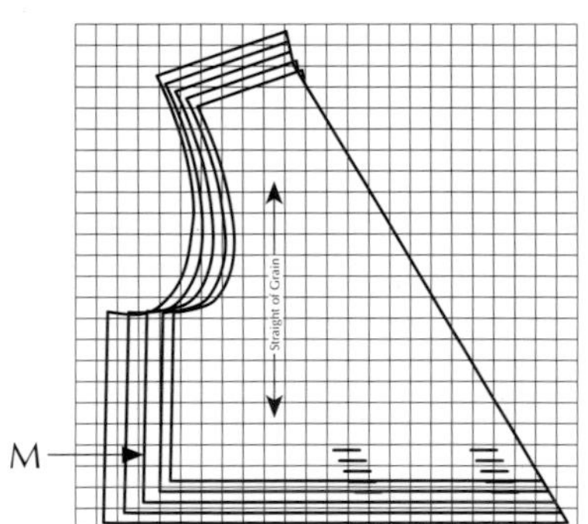

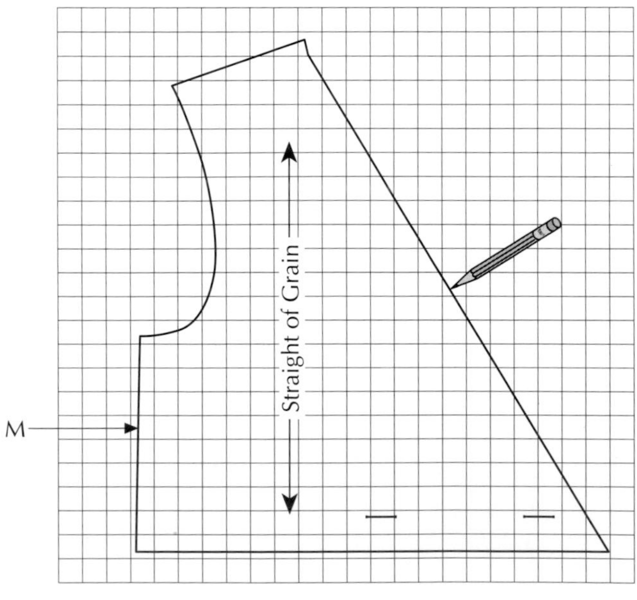

Latticework Vest

This vest is a great first-time chenille project. In the example shown here, the neutral-colored base fabric made just about any coloration possible for the chenille. The ceramic pansy buttons inspired the wonderful colors in the chenille latticework. Directions for making this vest begin on page 53.

Latticework Jacket

Denims make this jacket casual, but the touch of gold lamé adds elegance. Directions for making this jacket begin on page 62.

Handbag

Layered-and-stitched remnants can be put to good use on the flap of a handbag. You'll find suggestions for making use of leftover chenille strips on page 67.

Pillow

Here's another good use for leftover chenille strips.

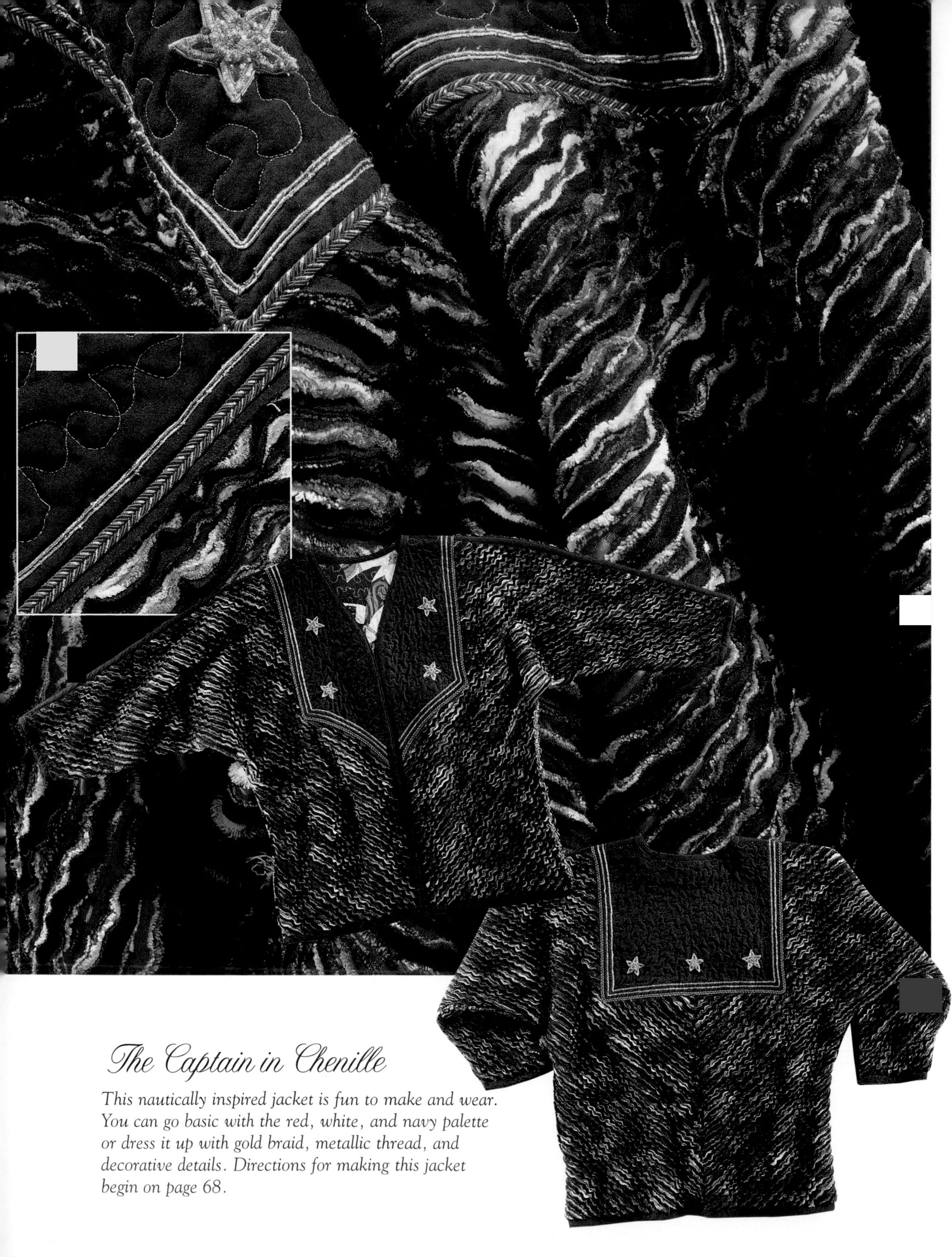

The Captain in Chenille

This nautically inspired jacket is fun to make and wear. You can go basic with the red, white, and navy palette or dress it up with gold braid, metallic thread, and decorative details. Directions for making this jacket begin on page 68.

Midnight Cowgirl

A different color palette, an alternate shape for the yoke, and a longer length make this jacket dramatically different from "The Captain in Chenille."

For this jacket, I selected a range of prints and solids in colorations from solid black for layers #1 and #6, and fabrics with pale gray and turquoise for the remaining layers. I also included a layer of silver lamé.

Cut five inches longer than "The Captain in Chenille," the length of this jacket provides a dressier look. I changed the shape of the yoke and embellished and bound the edges with Ultra Suede trim for a Western feel.

The change of direction in the stitching gives the chenille a herringbone look. Silver metallic thread wound in the bobbin sets off the rows of stitching on the lining.

Sawtooth Wall Hanging

42" x 42"

This wall hanging combines the traditional beauty and geometrics of a quilt pattern with the rich look of chenille. Who could resist curling up and snoozing under a slightly larger version? Directions for making this wall hanging begin on page 80.

The Puzzler

33" x 28"

The chenille pieces in this "jigsaw puzzle" fit together to make intriguing patterns. Because the pieces are cut from templates, the orientation of the stitching rows differs from piece to piece, creating interesting combinations of texture and shadow. Directions for making this wall hanging begin on page 86.

Latticework Vest

Color photo on page 47.

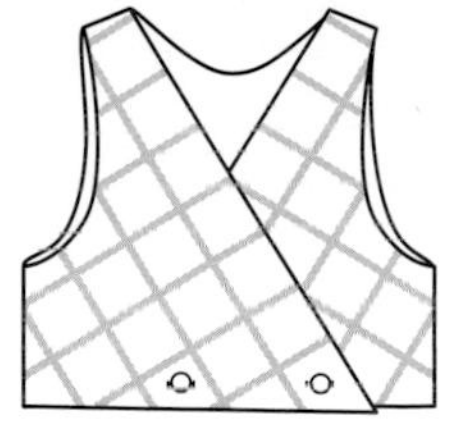

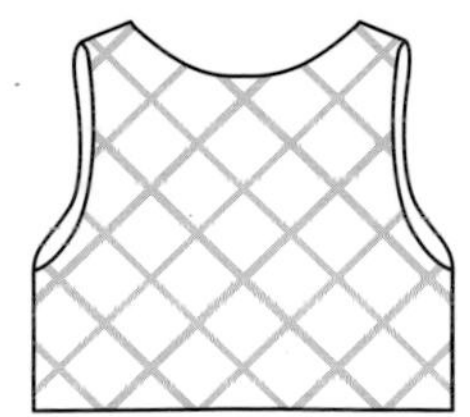

Latticework Vest Back

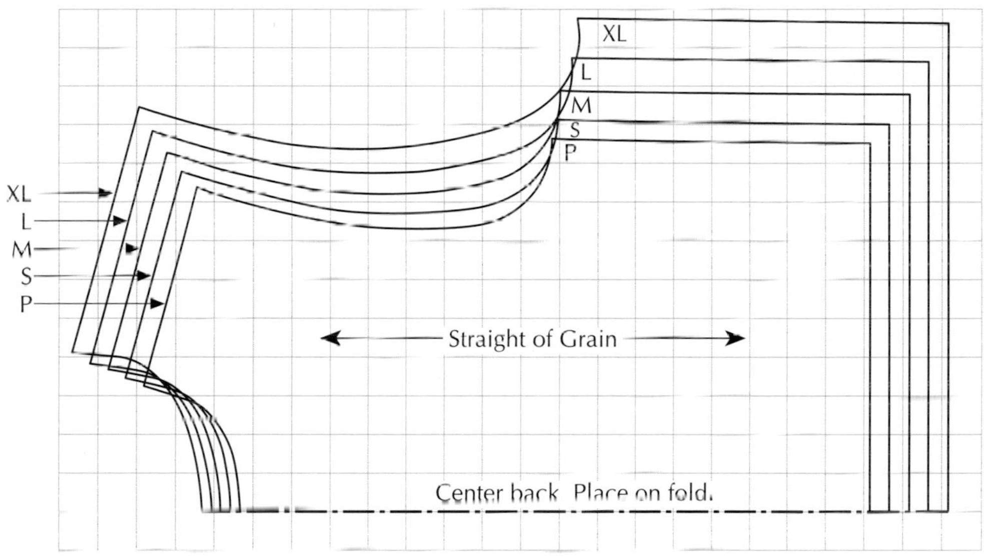

1 square = 1"

Latticework Vest Front

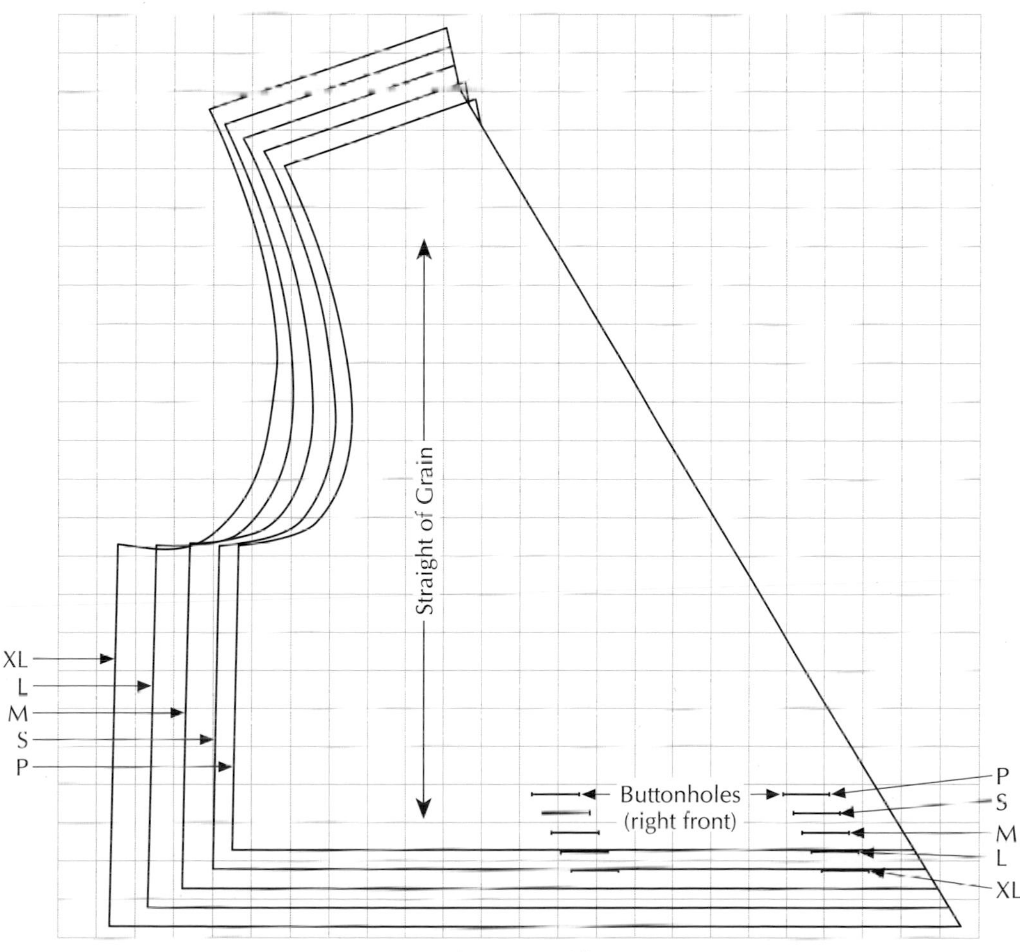

1 square = 1"

Cutting Layouts for Latticework Vest

Selvages

42"- to 45"-wide fabric,
sizes petite, small,
and medium

Front

Back

Lengthwise fold

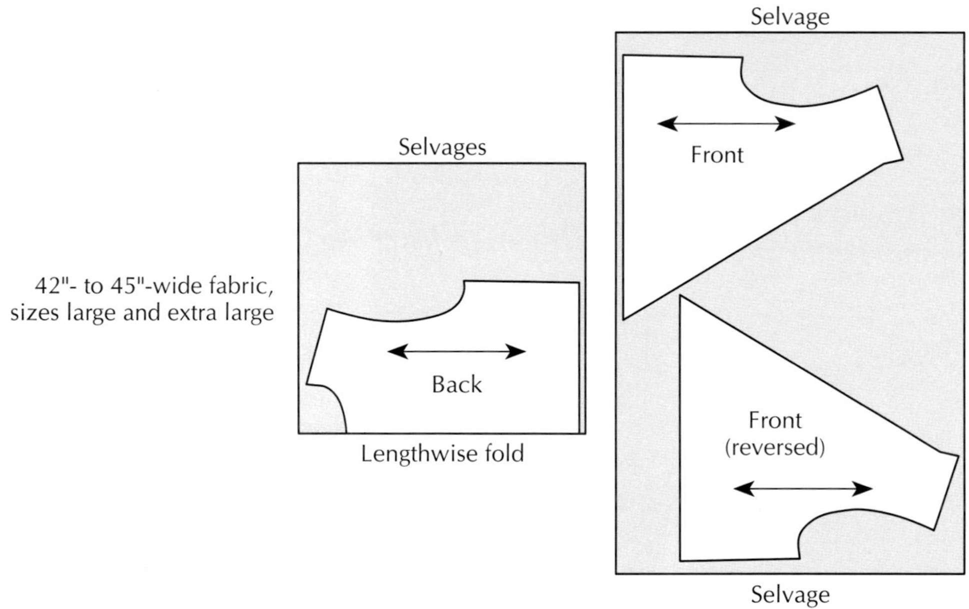

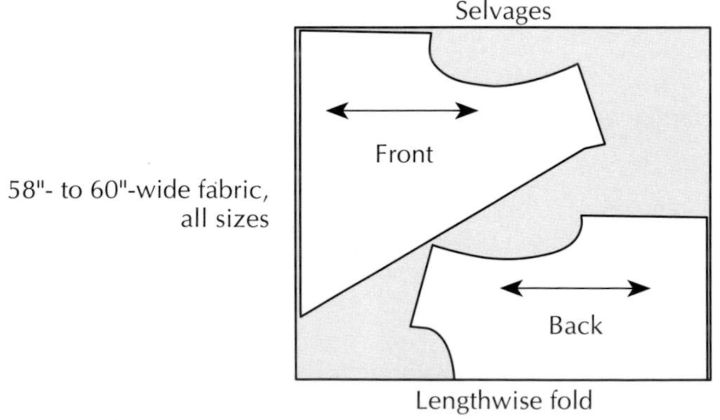

Fabric Selection

Refer to the suggestions for fabric selection on pages 7–24, and use a fabric for your base layer that has a stable weave. Denims or medium-weight cottons, such as cotton jacquard or poplin, are nice. Choose a fabric that will support the strips and won't shrink when washed and dried. A backing fabric that is too lightweight will pull up and distort when the strips are added and will not hold up well after being washed. The ideal base fabric will be wrinkle-free after washing and drying; fabric with some polyester content is an excellent choice. The chenille latticework will make it difficult to press the finished project.

I tried several combinations of fabrics for the lattice, selecting dusty rose, blues, lavenders, and yellows with off-whites that matched the base fabric. I chose colors that would blend to coordinate with the buttons. The photo above shows two of the colorations I tried. The photo below shows the final selection, with fabrics in the order they are stacked in the block.

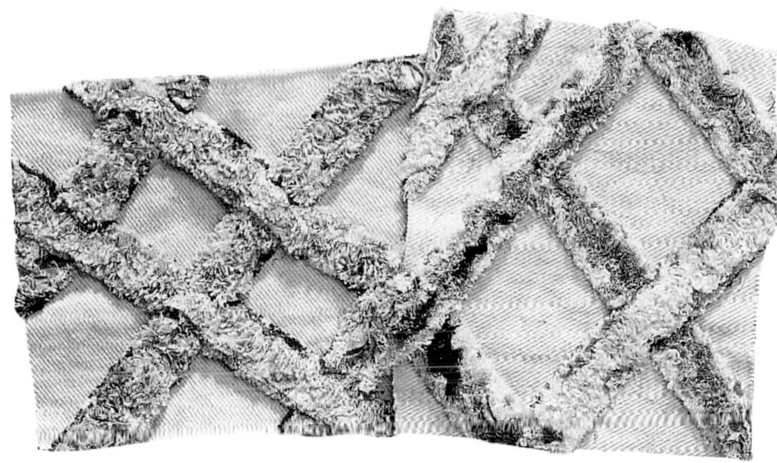

These sample squares show different colorations I tried when stacking the fabrics for the vest.

This lovely button provided inspiration for the chenille strips.

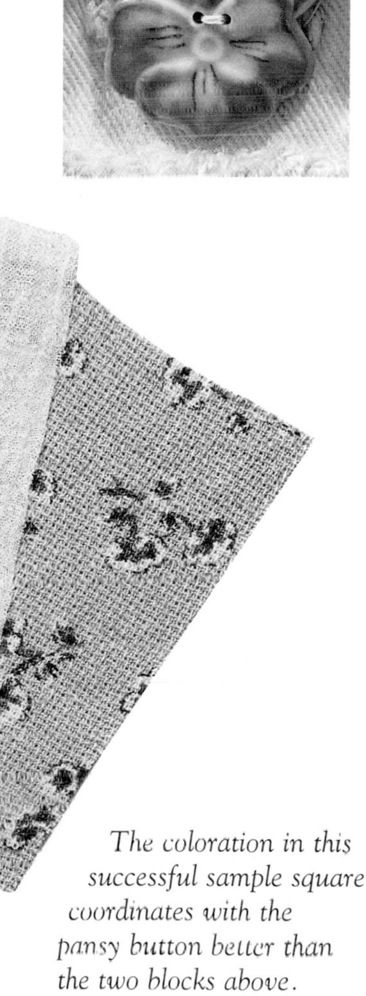

The coloration in this successful sample square coordinates with the pansy button better than the two blocks above.

Materials

Note: Do not prewash any of your fabrics.

Yardage Requirements			
Vest Size	**Fabric**	**42" to 45" wide**	**58" to 60" wide**
Petite	Base	1⅛ yds.	¾ yd.
	Lining	1⅛ yds.	¾ yd.
	Chenille lattice strips	⅓ yd. *each* of 5 fabrics	¼ yd. *each* of 5 fabrics
Small	Base	1⅛ yds.	⅞ yd.
	Lining	1⅛ yds.	⅞ yd.
	Chenille lattice strips	⅓ yd. *each* of 5 fabrics	¼ yd. *each* of 5 fabrics
Medium	Base	1⅛ yds.	⅞ yd.
	Lining	1⅛ yds.	⅞ yd.
	Chenille lattice strips	⅓ yd. *each* of 5 fabrics	¼ yd. *each* of 5 fabrics
Large	Base	2 yds.	1 yd.
	Lining	2 yds.	1 yd.
	Chenille lattice strips	⅓ yd. *each* of 5 fabrics	¼ yd. *each* of 5 fabrics
Extra-large	Base	2 yds.	1 yd.
	Lining	2 yds.	1 yd.
	Chenille lattice strips	⅓ yd. *each* of 5 fabrics	¼ yd. *each* of 5 fabrics
For all sizes, you need ⅝ yd. of fusible interfacing.			

Supplies

Refer to "General Supplies" on pages 6–7. In addition, you need:

- 2 fabulous buttons
- Thread that contrasts slightly with the top layer of fabric
- Bobbin thread that matches the base layer
- Optional: embellishments, such as buttons or beads, to place inside the latticed "windows" after the vest is finished

Assembling the Vest

1. Referring to "Sample Blocks" on pages 25–33, make sample blocks from your selected fabrics for the lattice strips. Select the best combination and number the layers from top (#1) to bottom (#5). The base layer will be #6.
2. Cut out the vest from the base fabric and lining, referring to the cutting layouts on page 54. Cut 2"-wide interfacing strips for the vest front and lower back. Using the vest back as a pattern, cut out 2"-wide back-neckline interfacing.

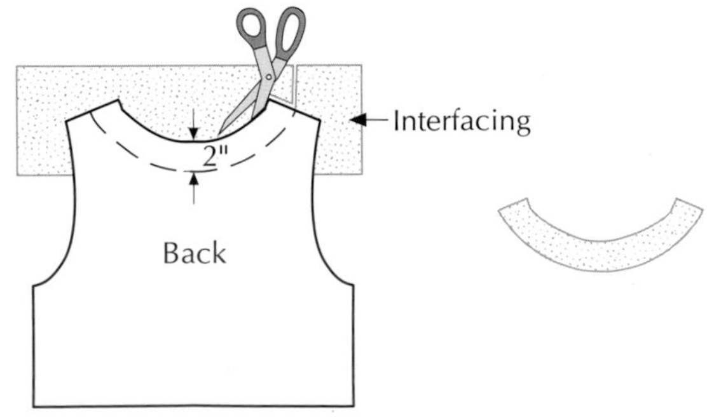

3. Following the manufacturer's directions, fuse the interfacing to the wrong sides of the vest fronts and to the back as shown.

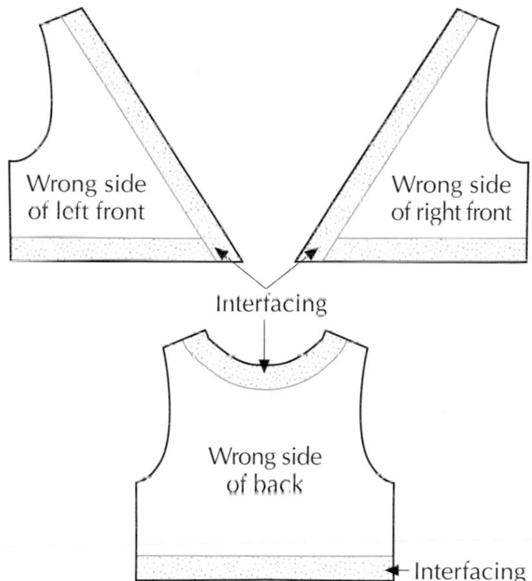

4. With right sides together, sew the vest fronts to the back at the shoulders. Repeat for the lining pieces. Press the seam allowances open.

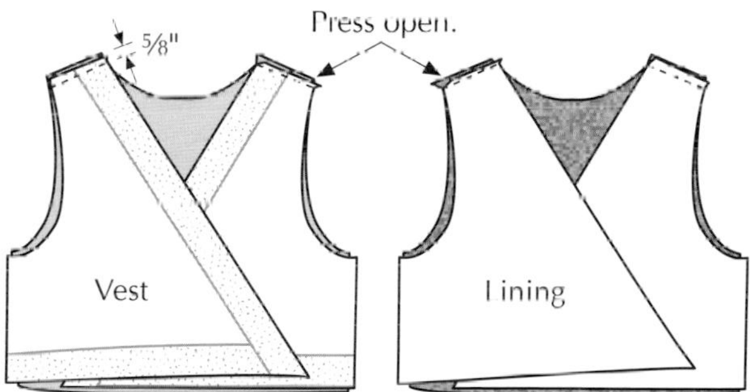

5. With right sides together, sew the vest to the lining at the armholes and neck. Stitch the lower edges, starting and stopping 2" from each side. Trim the seam allowances to ¼"; clip across corners to reduce bulk and clip curves as shown. Take care not to cut into the stitching.

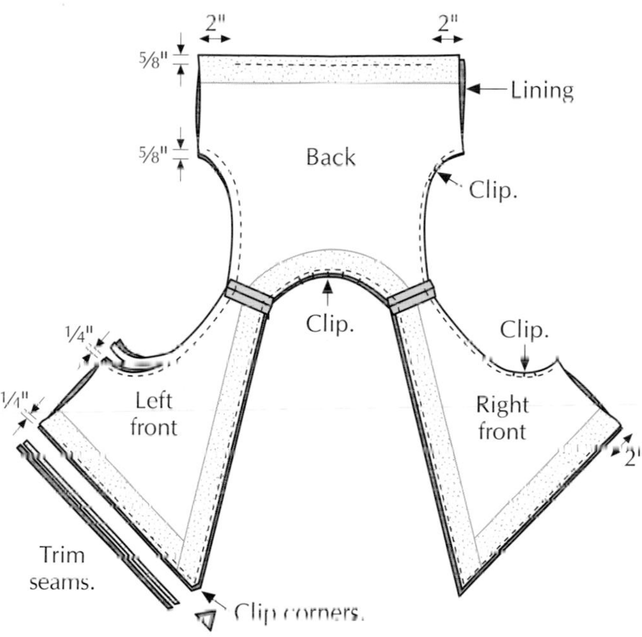

6. Turn the vest right side out, pulling each front through its shoulder and out the side opening. Press the underarm, neck, and lower seams.

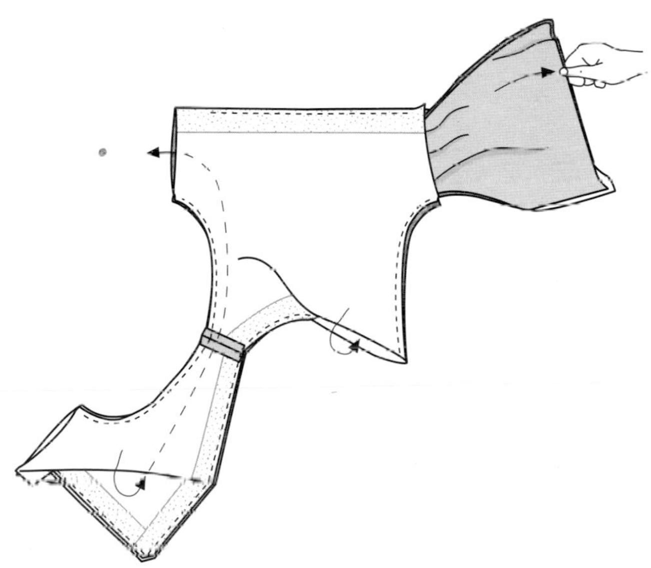

7. Pin the front and back at the sides, right sides together, matching the lower edges and armhole seams. Keep the lining free as you pin. Stitch just to the armhole seam (where it joins the lining).

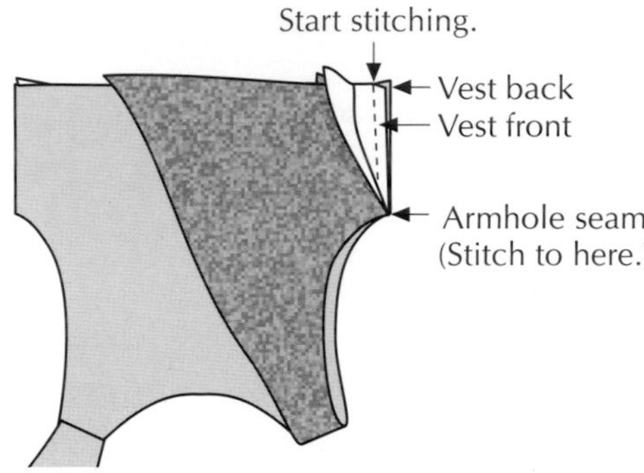

8. Pin the lining pieces together and stitch. Backstitch, then remove the garment from the machine. You should have a continuous seam that joins the vest front and back and the lining front and back at the sides. Press the seam allowances open. Repeat steps 7 and 8 for the remaining side.

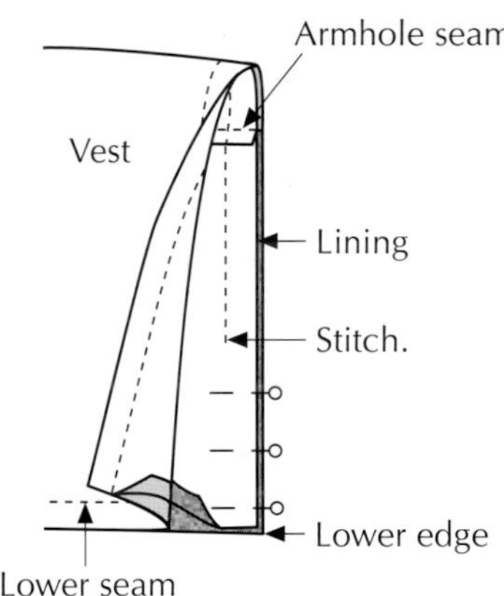

Note: It's possible to stitch the sides in one continuous seam, pinning and stitching the vest seam first, then pinning the lining just before stitching it. Take care not to catch the vest in the seam or stretch the fabrics as you sew.

9. Turn the vest to the right side, turning in the lower edges of the vest and lining at the sides. Press. Slipstitch the openings.

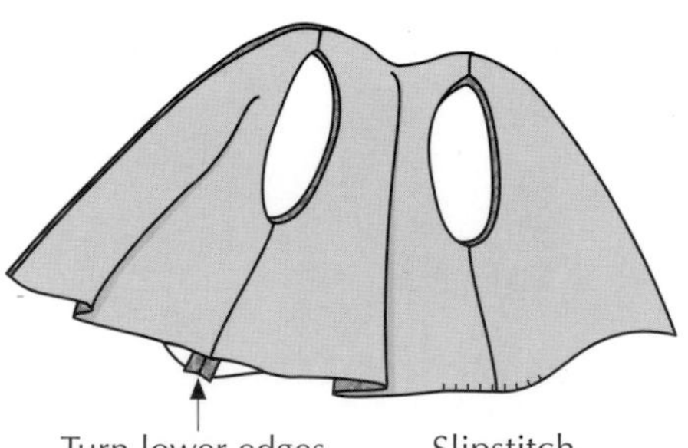

Drawing Lattice Placement Lines

The base for the vest is complete. It's time to apply the strips for the chenille lattice.

1. On the right front, mark the placement lines for the chenille strips with tailor's chalk. Mark the first line 3" from the front edge. Continue marking parallel lines, each 3" apart, across the vest front. Repeat for the left front.

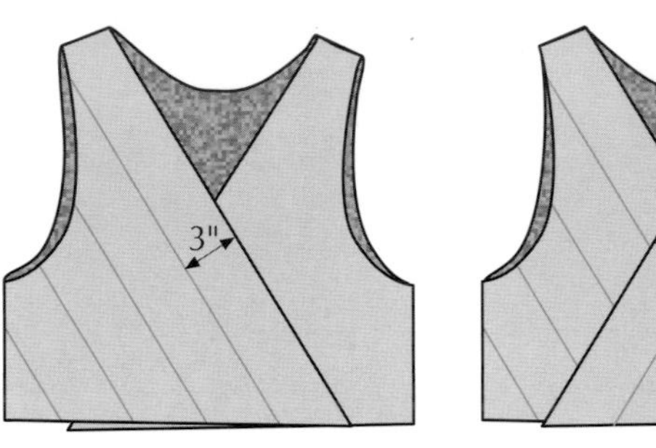

2. On the right front, align a Bias Square ruler with the front edge, placing the 4" mark at the lower point. Draw a line along the edge of the Bias Square. Continue drawing parallel lines, each 3" apart, working toward the shoulder. Repeat for the left front.

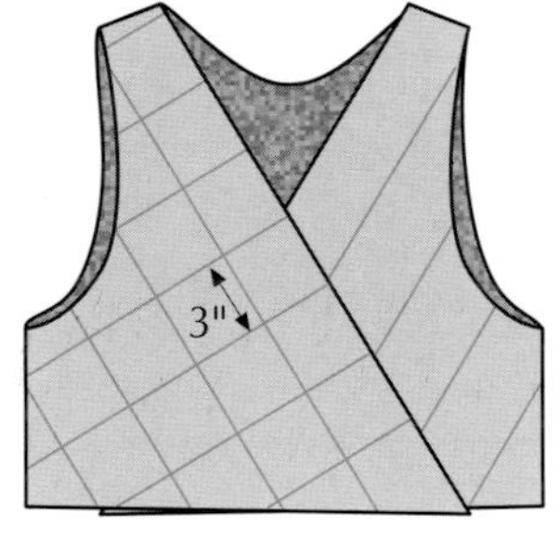

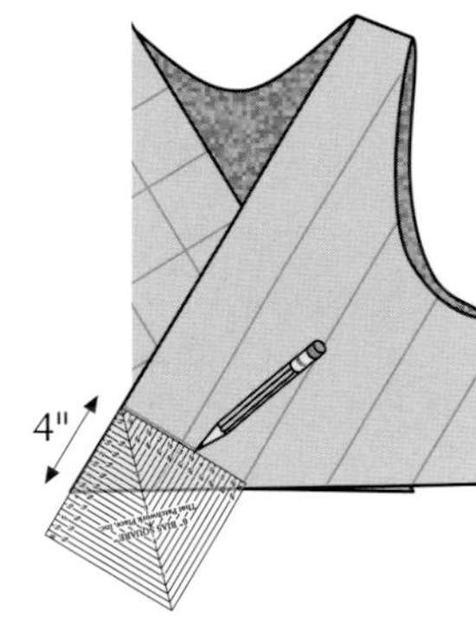

3. Fold the vest back in half to find the center and mark with tailor's chalk. Align the 45°-angle line on the Bias Square with the center line. Slide a ruler along the edge of the Bias Square to continue the line from the front section at a shoulder seam. Mark the line, maintaining the 45° angle. To each side of the first line draw parallel lines, 3" apart.

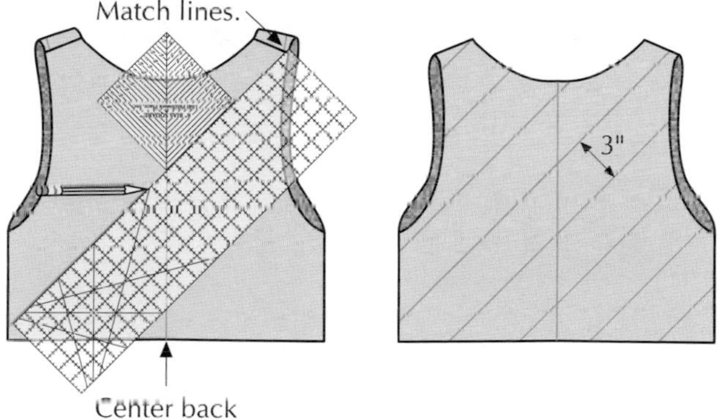

4. Continue the line from the front section at the other shoulder seam, as you did in step 3, making the lines perpendicular to the ones you just drew. Matching lines from front to back will create perfect diamonds down the back.

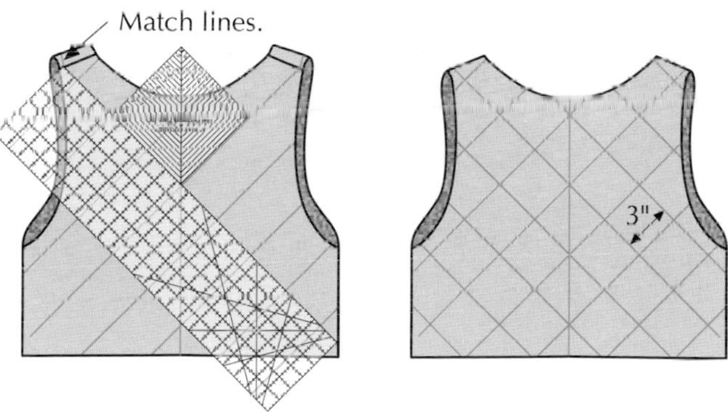

Preparing the Lattice Strips

1. Stack the chenille lattice-strip fabrics, right sides up, according to the order of your sample block. Place layers #1–#4 on top of layer #5. Pin around the edges and once every 4" across the entire surface. Pinning allows you to handle the layers as though they were a single piece of fabric.

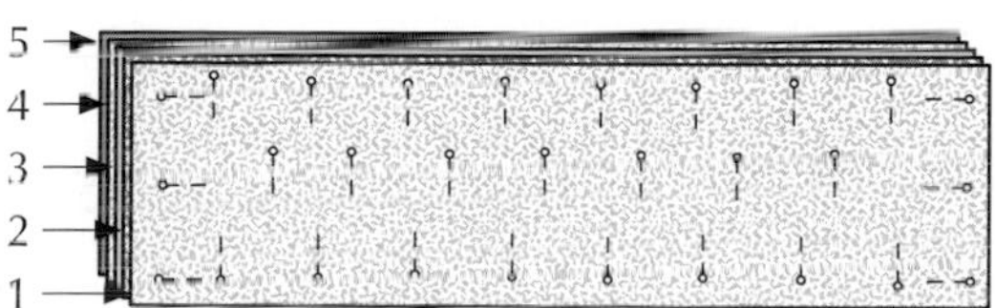

2. Align the 45°-angle line of an acrylic ruler with a long edge of the stack. Draw a diagonal line across the stack with tailor's chalk or with a marking pencil.

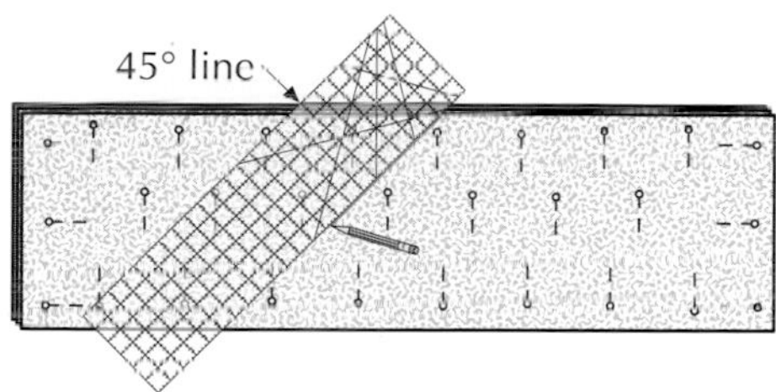

3. Sew along the 45°-angle line. Continue stitching rows ⅝" apart on one side of the first stitching line until you reach the corner. Continue sewing rows on the other side of the first stitching line until the entire stack is quilted.

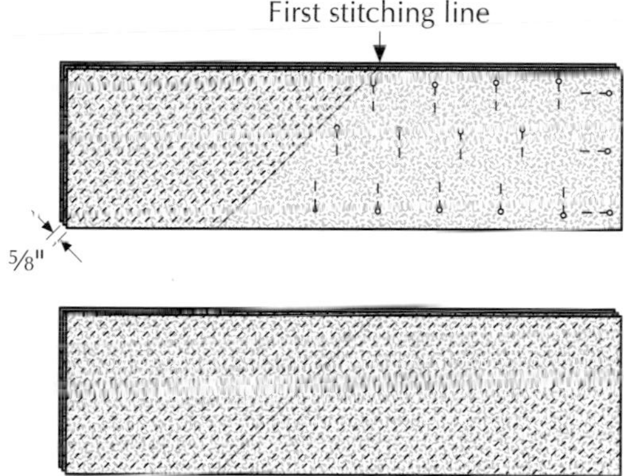

4. Place the quilted stack on the cutting mat. Using a rotary cutter, carefully cut between each row of stitching, *through all the layers*. Each strip should have approximately ¼" of fabric on each side of the stitching. See the Tip on page 60.

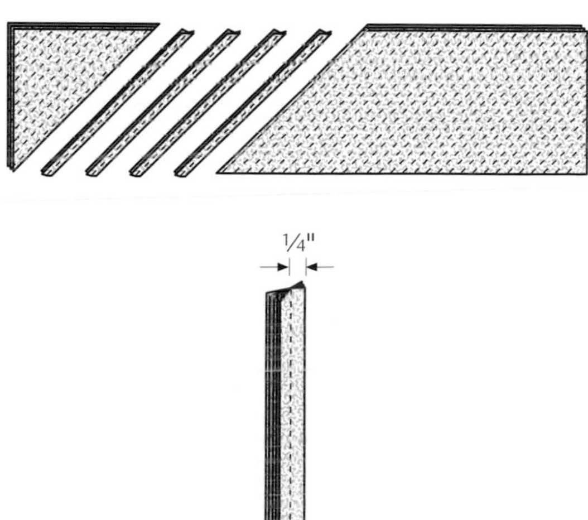

Tip

WHEN CUTTING THE STRIPS FOR CHENILLE, CUT THE LONG CENTER STRIPS FIRST, AS YOU NEED THEM. THE STITCHED, UNCUT CORNER PIECES KEEP BETTER THAN CUT STRIPS. CUT THE CORNER PIECES INTO SHAPES OR STRIPS AS NEEDED FOR OTHER PROJECTS.

Sewing Strips to the Vest

1. Beginning with the first placement line of one front section, center a chenille strip's stitching line over the placement line. Sew over the chenille strip's stitching, through all thicknesses. Sew the remaining parallel strips to the vest front.

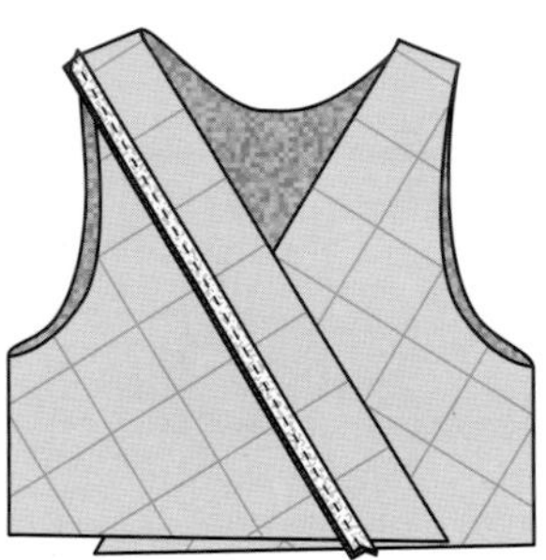

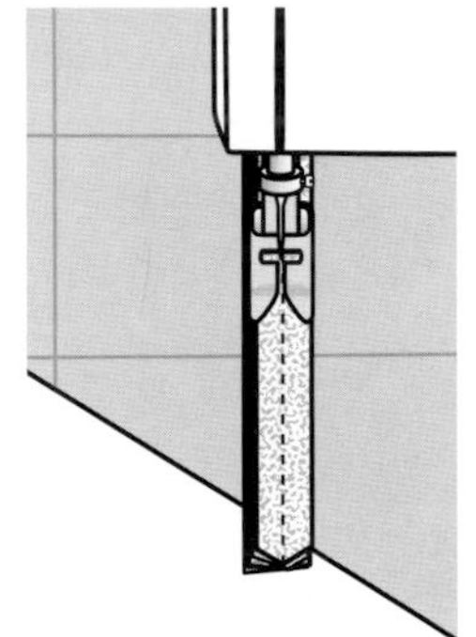

2. Sew parallel strips across the remaining front section, then sew parallel strips to the back. Sew the perpendicular strips to the vest front and back, crossing the previously sewn strips.

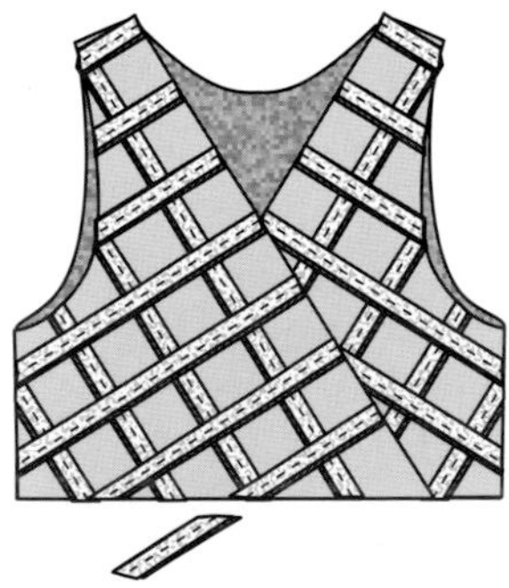

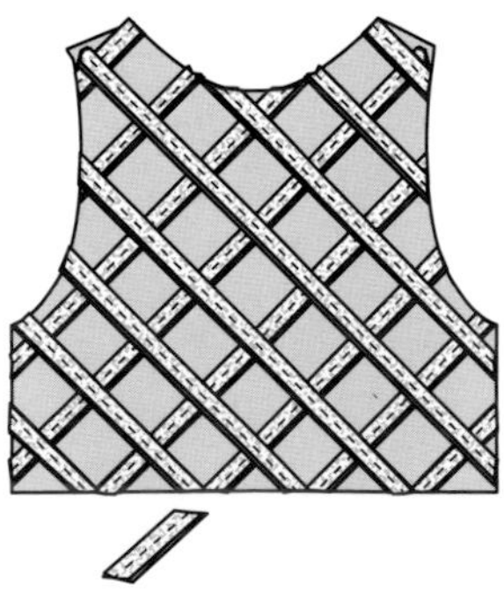

Note: *If the strips are too short to reach each end of the line, make a perpendicular cut at the end of the strip. Overlap it slightly with the perpendicular end of the next strip and continue stitching. After washing, these joints won't show.*

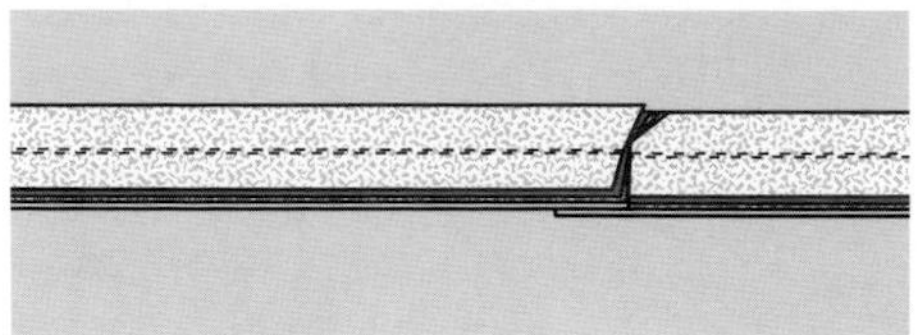

When sewing chenille strips to the vest, cut the ends of each strip at the same angle as the edge or seam where it ends.

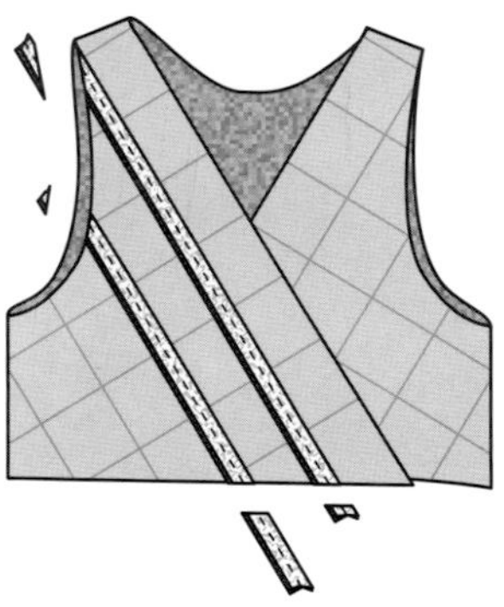

To reduce bulk, don't continue a long strip over the shoulder or side seams. Place the end of the strip about 1/8" from the seam line and start another strip on the other side of the seam to continue the lattice.

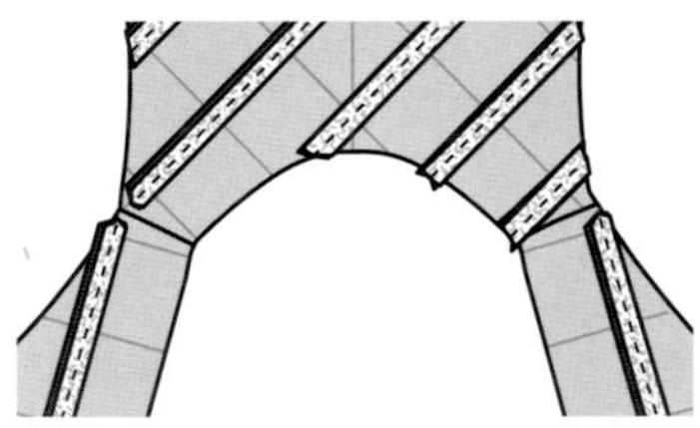

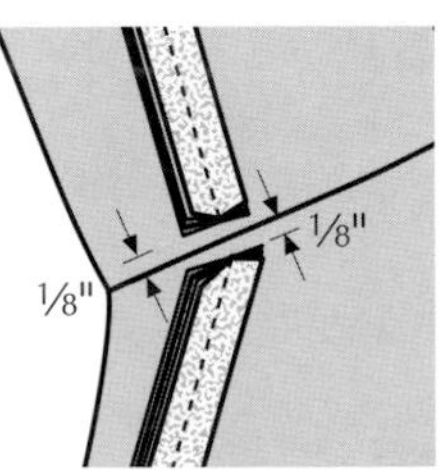

3. Make buttonholes in the right vest front as shown. Center the buttonholes inside the "windows" of chenille latticework, taking care to allow for the ⅝"-wide chenille row you will place at the lower edge.

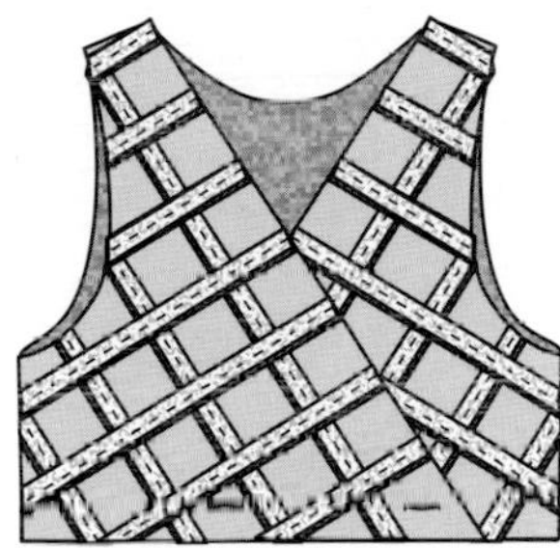

4. Center strips over the shoulder and side seams and stitch in place.

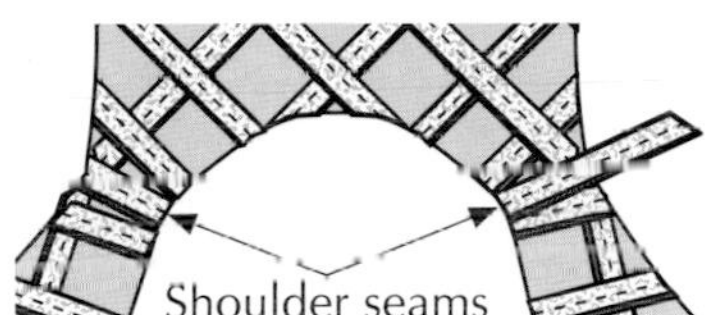

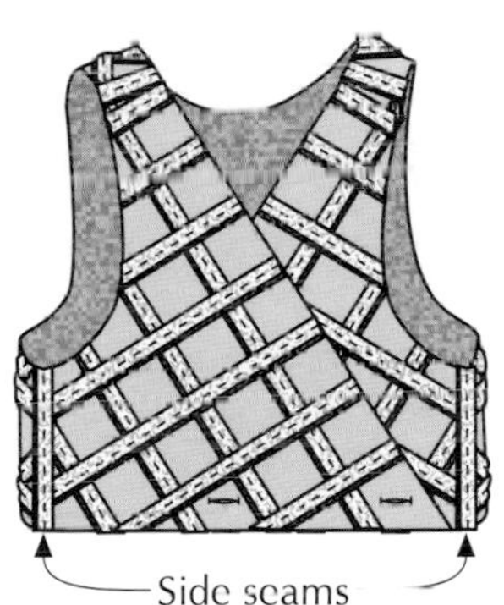

5. Starting at a side seam, center a chenille strip's stitching line about ⅛" from the lower edge. Stitch in place. Continue adding strips, moving up the vest front, around the neck, then down again until you reach your starting point. Add more strips to the armholes to finish.

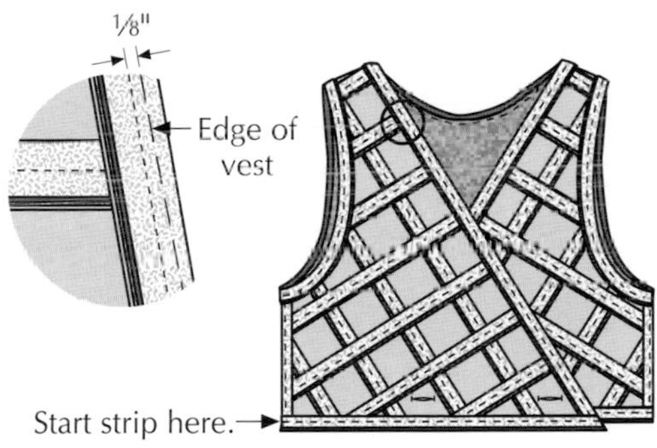

Note: At the corners and under the armhole, cut and overlap the ends rather than turning them. (See the Note on page 60.)

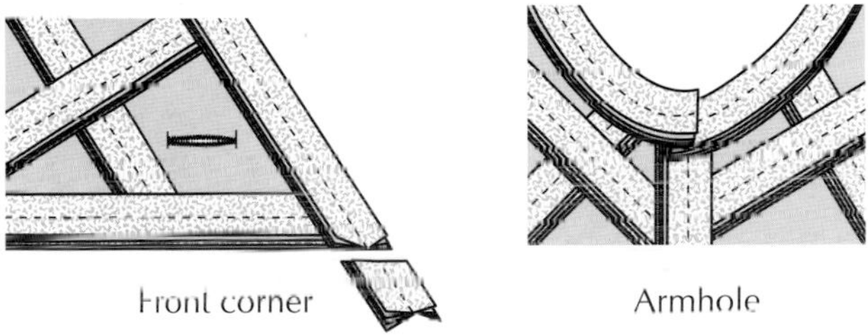

Finishing

It's time to throw your vest in the washing machine! Refer to "Laundering Chenille" on pages 32–33. After your vest has been washed and dried, sew buttons to the front.

The latticework windows are perfect places for all those wonderful embellishment techniques you've learned over the years. Embellishments can be as simple as buttons, beads, or metallic studs, or as elaborate as suede fabric leaves and vines accented with silk-ribbon roses.

Latticework Jacket

Color photo on page 48.

Adding sleeves to the Latticework Vest turns it into a great jacket. The chenille strips on the sleeves are spaced 4" apart, and the strips on the body are 3" apart. The jacket is completely lined.

For this jacket I selected a denimlike fabric for the base and a combination of the base fabric, cotton gauze, and metallic madras plaid for the chenille strips. For more ideas, refer to the suggestions for fabric selection on pages 7–24 and on page 55.

Note: For the jacket front and back, use the pattern grids for the vest front and back on page 53.

Latticework Jacket Sleeve

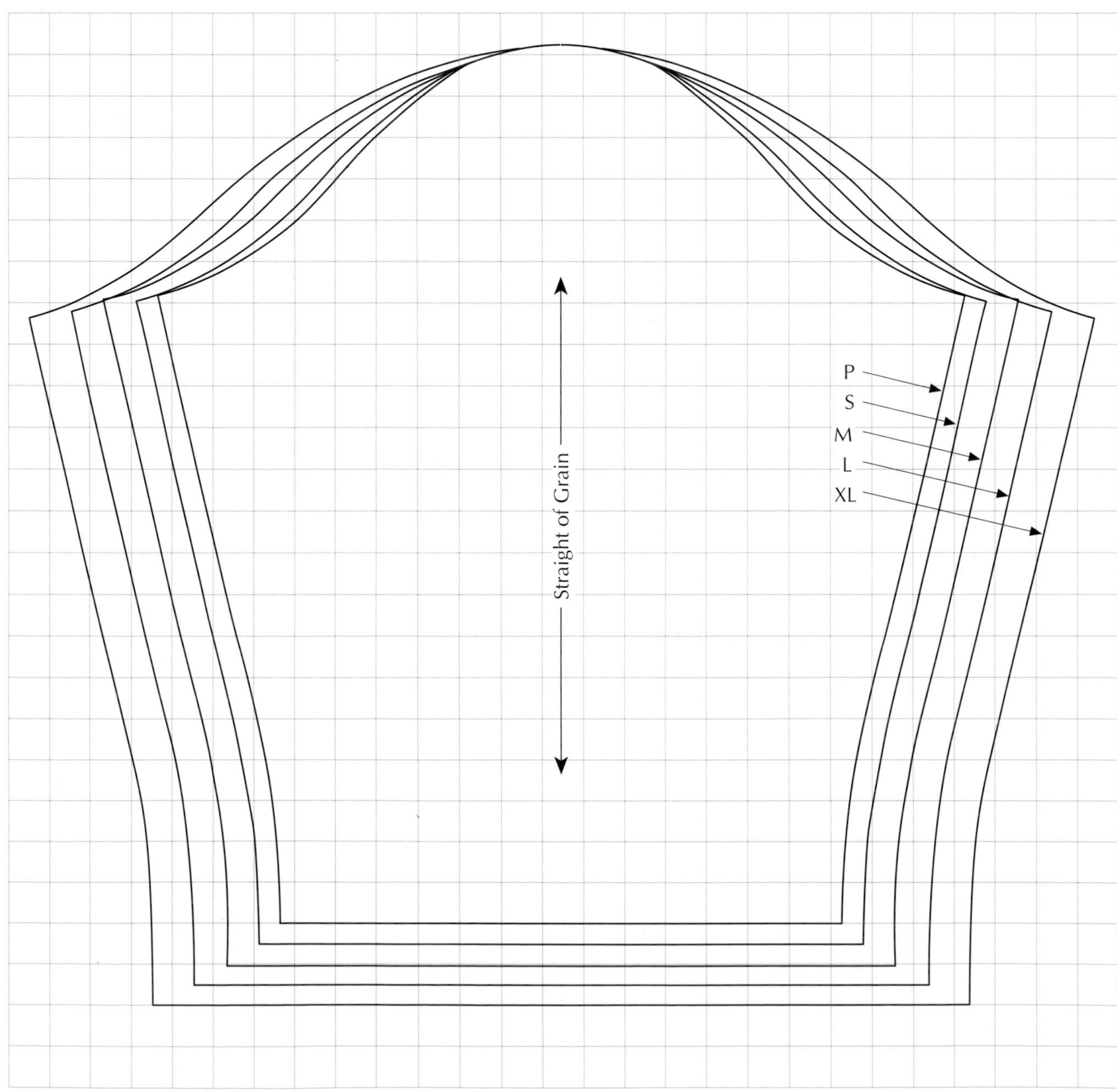

1 square = 1"

Materials

Note: Do not prewash any of your fabrics.

Yardage Requirements			
Jacket Size	**Fabric**	**42" to 45" wide**	**58" to 60" wide**
Petite	Base	1½ yds.	1½ yds.
	Lining	1½ yds.	1½ yds.
	Chenille lattice strips	½ yd. *each* of 5 fabrics	⅓ yd. *each* of 5 fabrics
Small	Base	1¾ yds.	1⅝ yds.
	Lining	1¾ yds.	1⅝ yds.
	Chenille lattice strips	½ yd. *each* of 5 fabrics	⅓ yd. *each* of 5 fabrics
Medium	Base	2½ yds.	1¾ yds.
	Lining	2½ yds.	1¾ yds.
	Chenille lattice strips	½ yd. *each* of 5 fabrics	⅓ yd. *each* of 5 fabrics
Large	Base	2¾ yds.	1¾ yds.
	Lining	2¾ yds.	1¾ yds.
	Chenille lattice strips	½ yd. *each* of 5 fabrics	⅓ yd. *each* of 5 fabrics
Extra-large	Base	2⅞ yds.	1⅞ yds.
	Lining	2⅞ yds.	1⅞ yds.
	Chenille lattice strips	½ yd. *each* of 5 fabrics	⅓ yd. *each* of 5 fabrics
For all sizes, you need ⅝ yd. of fusible interfacing.			

Supplies

Refer to "General Supplies" on pages 6–7. In addition, you need:

- 2 fabulous buttons
- Thread that contrasts slightly with the top layer of fabric
- Bobbin thread that matches the base layer
- Optional: embellishments, such as buttons, beads, or enamel pins, to place inside the latticed "windows" after the jacket is finished

Prepare the Latticework Jacket pattern in your size, referring to "Preparing the Pattern" on page 46.

Cutting Layouts for Latticework Jacket

42"- to 45"-wide fabric, sizes petite and small
58"- to 60"-wide fabric, all sizes

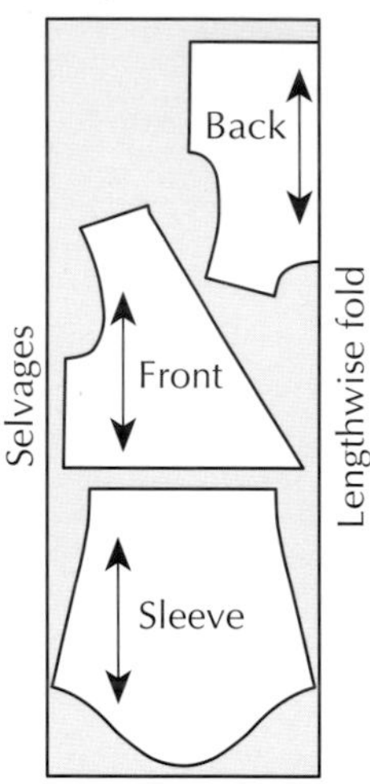

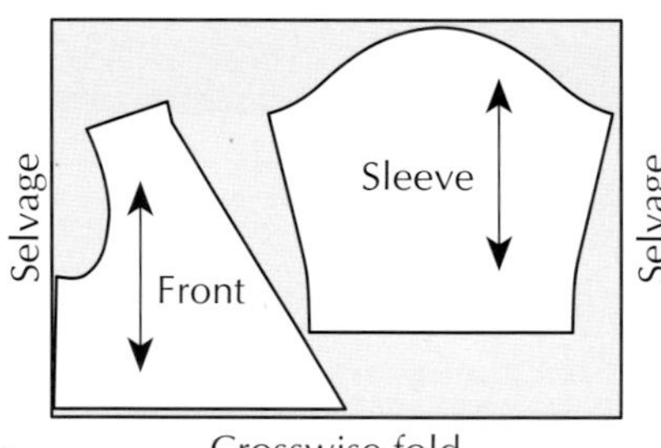

42"- to 45"-wide fabric, sizes medium, large, and extra large

Selvages

Back

Lengthwise fold

Assembling the Jacket

1. For the lattice strips, make sample blocks from your selected fabrics, referring to "Sample Blocks" on pages 25–33. Select the best combination and number the layers from top (#1) to bottom (#5). The base layer will be #6.
2. Cut out the jacket from the base fabric and linings, referring to the cutting layouts at left. Then follow steps 2–4 of "Assembling the Vest" on pages 56–57.
3. With right sides together, sew the jacket to the lining at the neck, front, and lower edges, then trim seam allowances to ¼" wide. Clip the neckline curve and across the front corners to reduce bulk. Turn the jacket right side out; press.

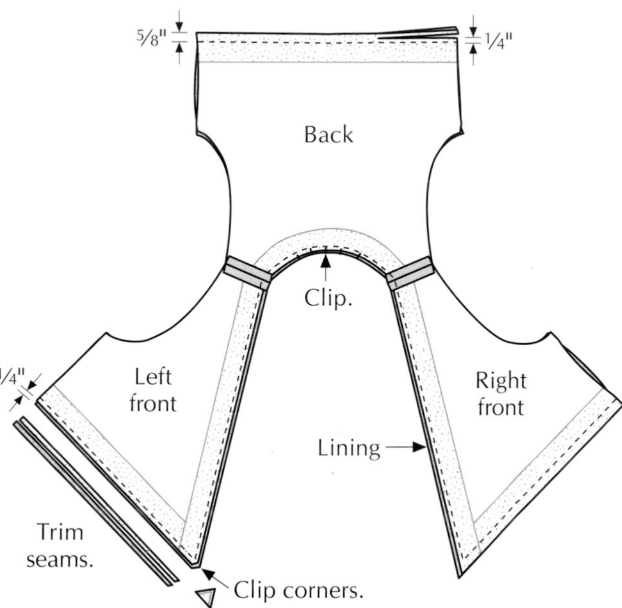

4. With right sides together and raw edges matching, sew the *unlined* sleeves to the jacket and lining at the armhole seams. Press the seam allowances toward the sleeves.

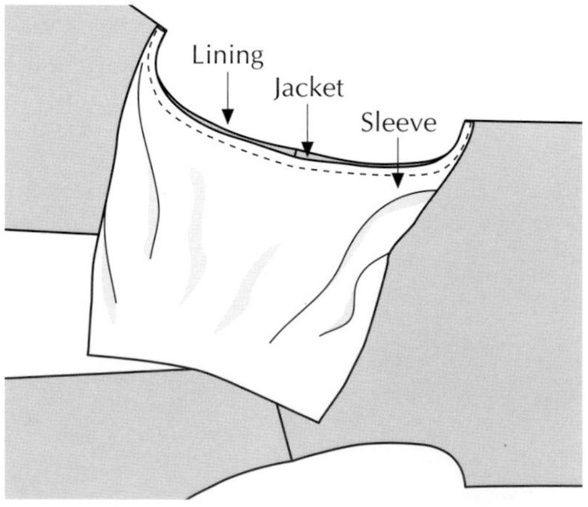

5. Referring to "Drawing Lattice Placement Lines" on pages 58–59, mark placement lines on the front and back of the jacket.
6. Mark diagonal placement lines on the sleeves, spacing them 4" apart. I started at the center of the sleeve cap, where it joins at the shoulder seam. I had to adjust the lines slightly to align them with the bodice placement lines.

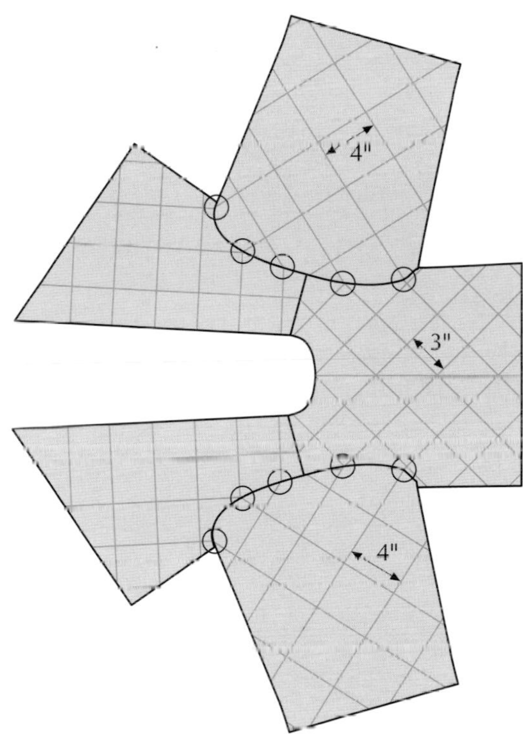

7. Referring to "Preparing the Lattice Strips" on page 59, make lattice strips for your jacket.
8. Follow steps 1–2 of "Sewing Strips to the Vest" and the Note on page 60, then stitch lattice strips to the sleeves at the shoulder and armhole seams.
9. With right sides together, sew the front and back together with 1 continuous seam, starting at the sleeve and ending at the lower edge. Treat the lining and jacket as 1 layer. Serge the seam, or stitch with a ⅝"-wide seam allowance, then trim the seam allowance to ¼" and finish the edges with a zigzag stitch.

10. Turn the jacket right side out. Stitch lattice strips to the side seams, stopping at the underarm seam.

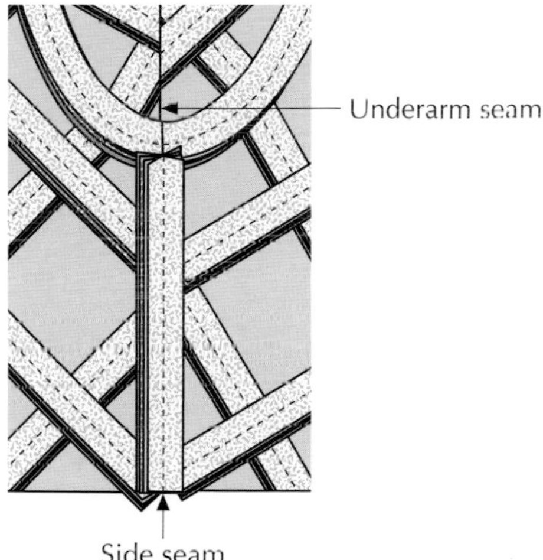

11. Using the lower edge of a sleeve as a pattern, cut a 3" wide facing from the base fabric for each sleeve.

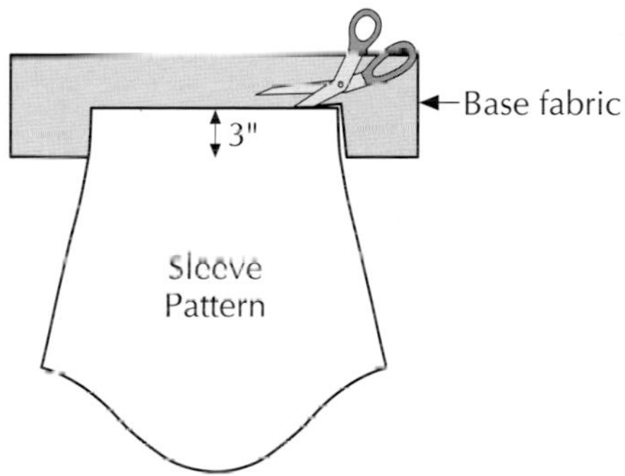

12. Cut 2¾"-wide interfacing strips. Following the manufacturer's directions, fuse the interfacing to the wrong side of the sleeve facings. Fold the facing in half as shown and stitch along the short edge. Press the seam allowances open.

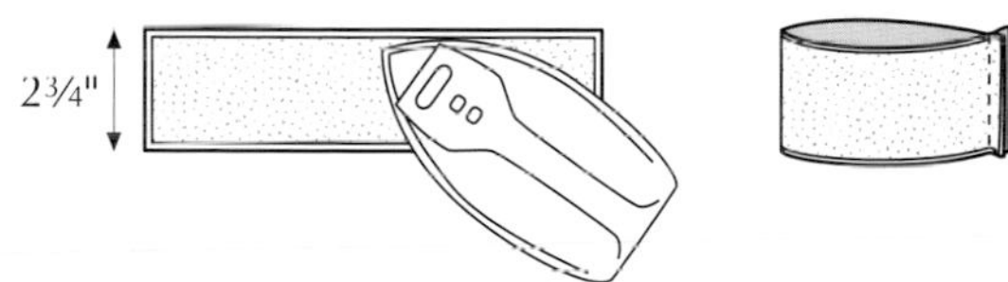

13. With right sides together and seams matching, sew a facing to the lower edge of a sleeve. Trim the seam allowance to ¼". Turn the facing right side out. Understitch by sewing next to the seam, through the sleeve and facing seam allowances to create a crisp sleeve turn. Turn the facing to the inside and press. Repeat for the other sleeve.

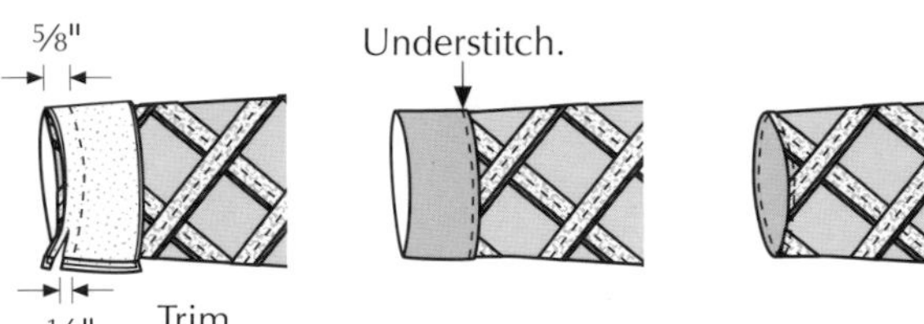

14. With right sides together, stitch each sleeve lining's underarm seam. Press the seam allowances open. Turn the sleeve right side out, then press under the ⅝"-wide seam allowance of the sleeve cap and lower edge.

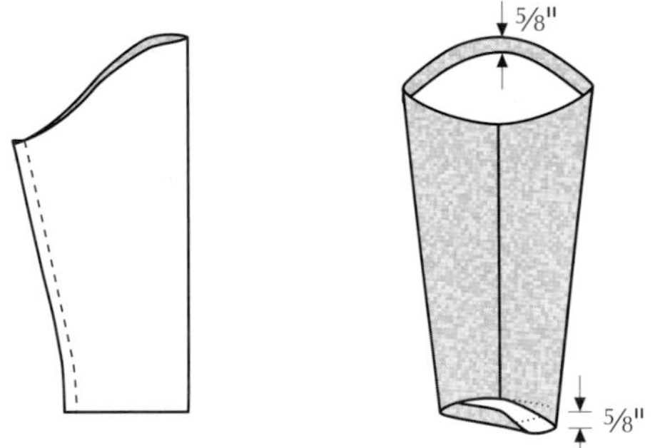

15. Turn the sleeve linings inside out. Matching underarm and armhole seams, pin the sleeve linings to the inside of the jacket at the sleeve cap and lower edges. Leave enough ease in the length at the lower edge to allow comfortable movement. Slipstitch securely.

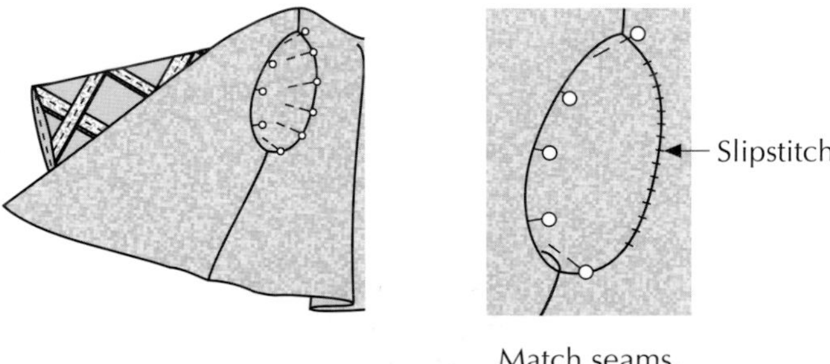

Match seams.

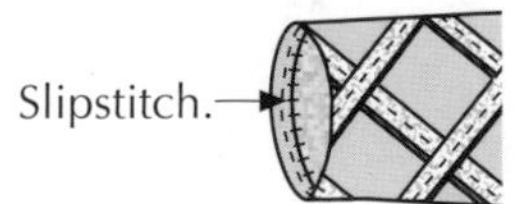

16. Make buttonholes on the right front. Center the buttonholes inside the "windows" of the chenille latticework, taking care to allow for the row of chenille that you will place around the edges of the jacket.

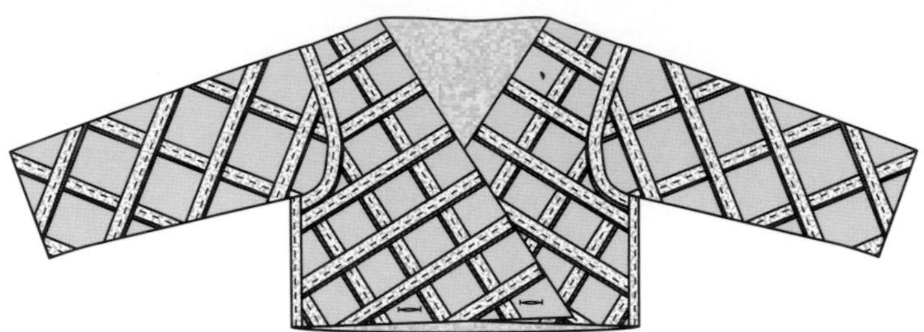

17. Starting at a side seam, center a chenille strip's stitching line about ⅛" from the lower edge. Stitch in place. Continue adding strips, moving up the jacket front, around the neck, then down again until you reach your starting point. Add strips to the lower edges of the sleeves to finish. (See the Notes on pages 60 and 61.)

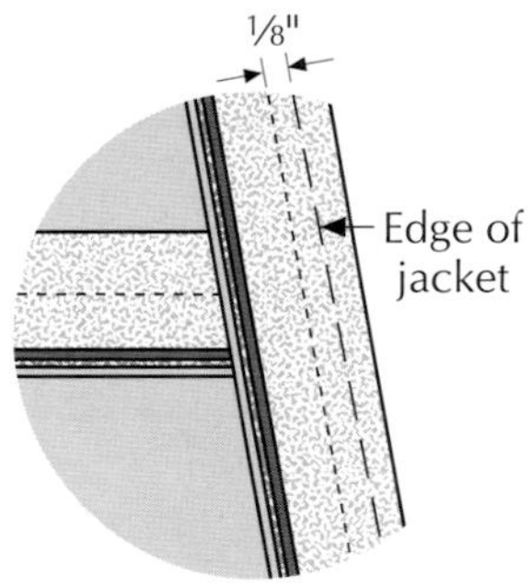

Finishing

Wash and dry your jacket, referring to "Laundering Chenille" on pages 32–33. Sew the buttons to the left front. See "Finishing" on page 61 for embellishment ideas.

Using Chenille Scraps

Leftover chenille strips should never go to waste. It doesn't take many strips to embellish a handbag or pillow. For these projects, use short lattice strips cut from corner pieces of layered-and-stitched rectangles. (See the Tip on page 60.)

Handbag

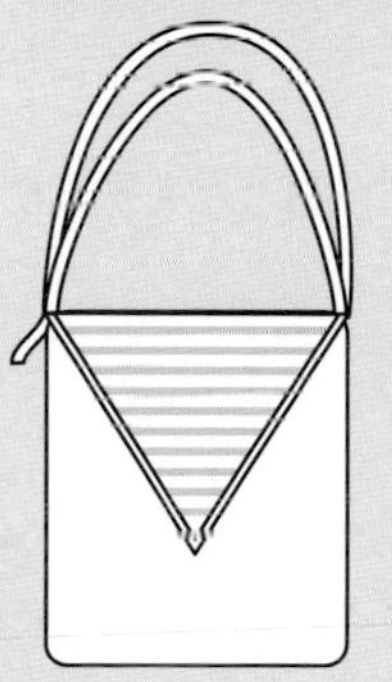

Leftover chenille strips, sewn to a backing, make an ideal flap for a handbag. Use base-fabric scraps to make the handbag's body, flap facing, and straps. For the flap, use the uncut corner of a layered-and-stitched rectangle you prepared for chenille strips. (See page 59.) Using your favorite handbag pattern, cut the layered corner into the shape of the flap. Sew over the original stitching to attach the strips to the flap facing, then slash the top layers, leaving the base fabric intact. Bind the flap and sew it to the body of the handbag, following the pattern instructions.

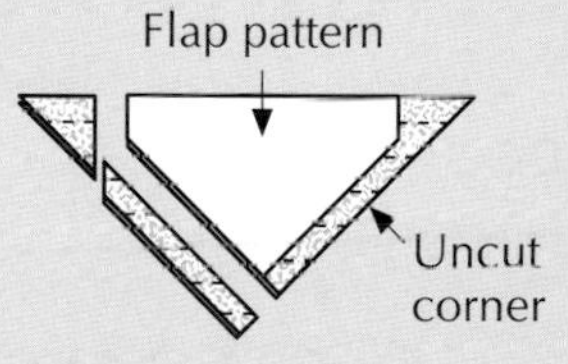

Cut out the flap.

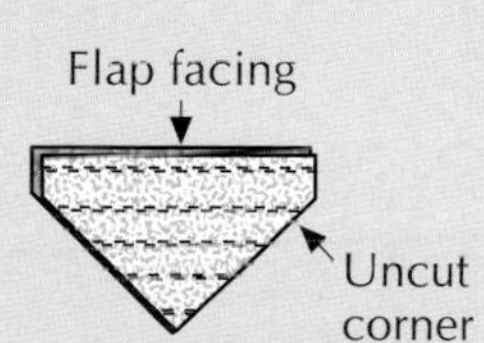

Stitch to flap facing.

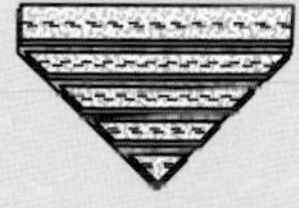

Slash.

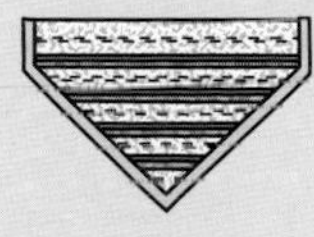

Bind.

Pillow

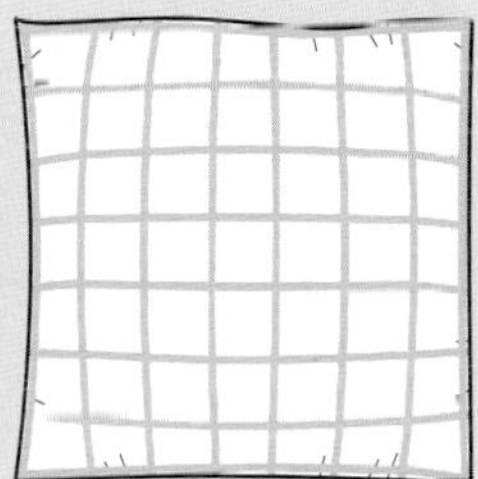

After making the Latticework Vest, I stitched the leftover chenille strips into a grid pattern for a pillow. I faced and turned the pillow top, then stitched another row of strips around the edge. I stuffed the pillow after washing and drying it.

If you still have strips left after all this, make a coin purse!

The Captain in Chenille

Color photo on page 50.

The Captain in Chenille Jacket Front

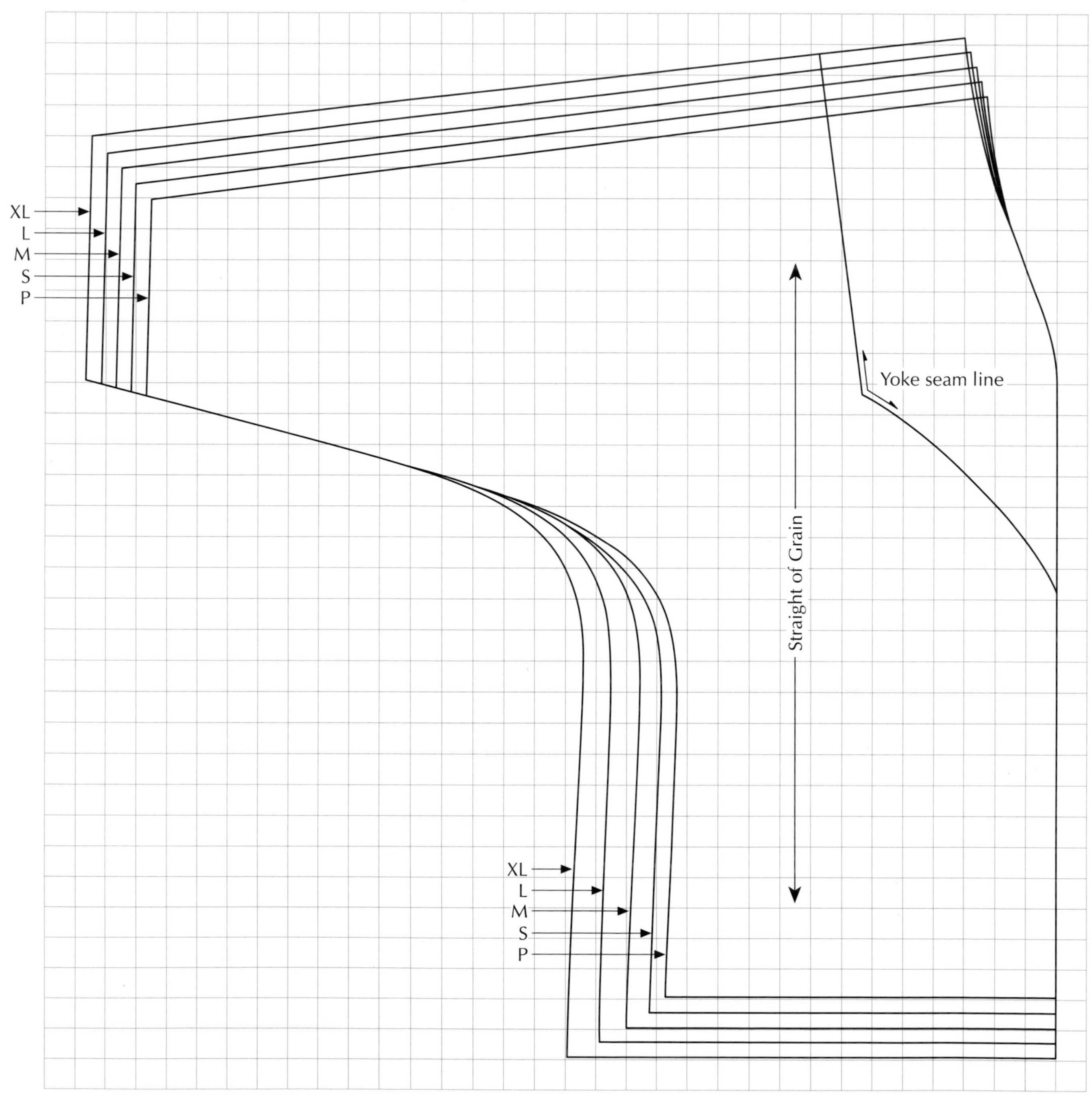

1 square = 1"

The Captain in Chenille Jacket Back

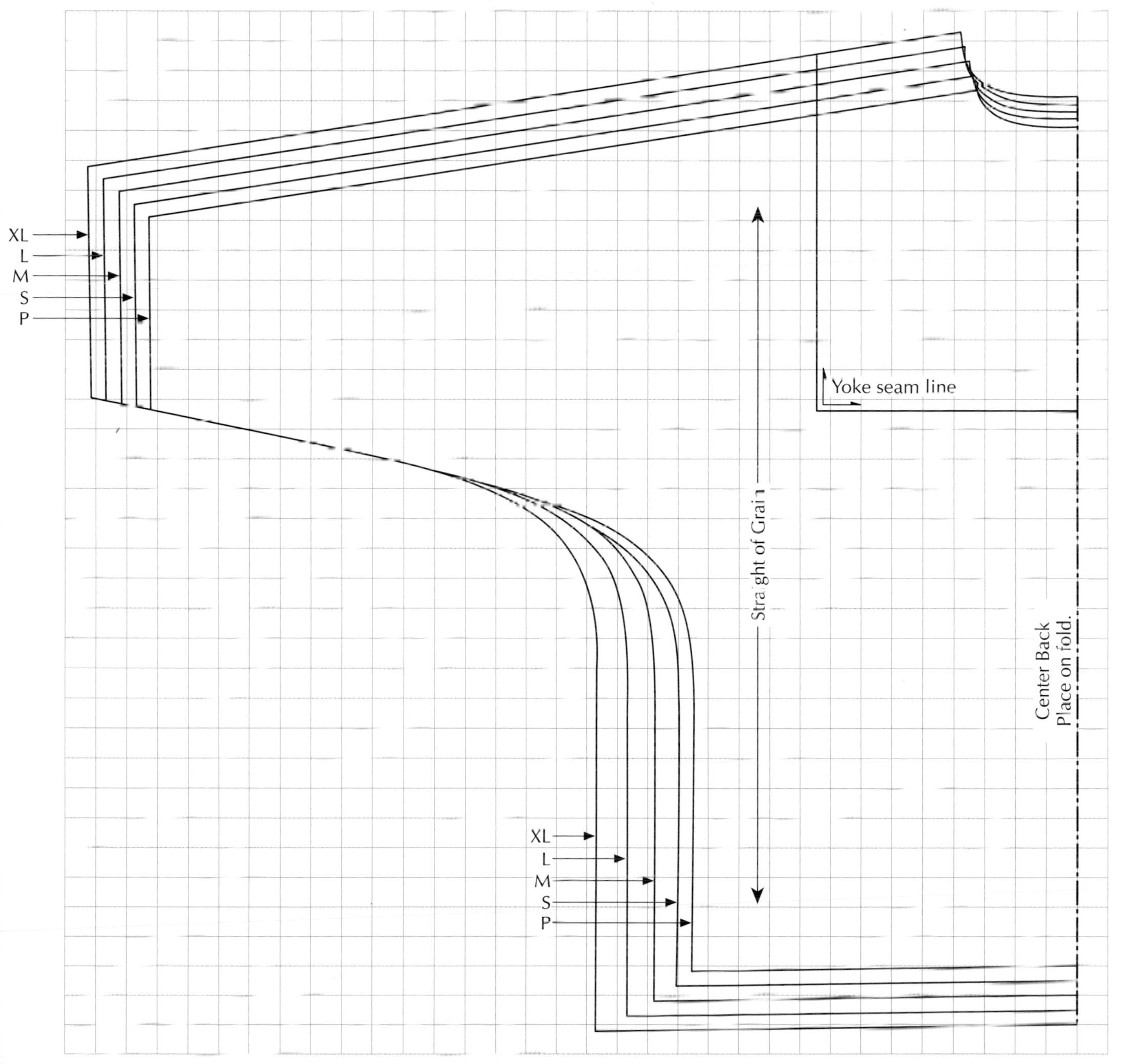

1 square = 1"

Cutting Layout for the Captain in Chenille

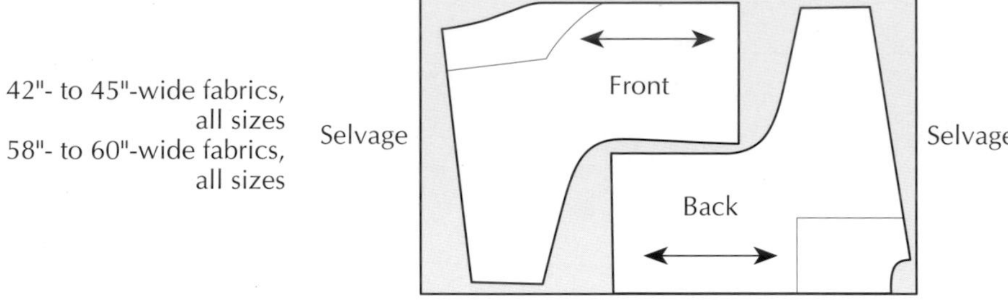

I like making chenille because it's usually fun, often humorous, and always surprising. The technique allows the maker to be less than perfect, unlike many wearable-art techniques that require precision and attention to detail. I know that if my rows of stitching are not perfect, if the fabrics cause me grief and create slight waves, I will still have a sumptuous result. The laundering process will conceal imperfections, so if my finishing work is up to par, the rest will take care of itself.

After the work is finished and laundered, I am always anxious to show off the garment to my family. Even though I made sample squares, it's not until I take the garment out of the dryer that I see the full effect of the fabric combinations.

Wanting this jacket to have a nautical feel and coloration, I spent a great deal of time layering my red, white, and blue fabrics and perfecting the detailing of the yoke area with embroidery and nautical-looking trims. After I took the jacket from the dryer, I ran downstairs to present the finished product to my husband. I told him this one-of-a-kind jacket needed a nautical name. After I suggested a few names that I thought would be good, my husband studied the jacket for a few minutes and said, "I know, I know—it has to be 'The Captain in Chenille!'"

Fabric Selection

Refer to the suggestions for fabric selection on pages 7–24. I used 100% rayon solids and prints.

Select red, white, blue, and bright colors in prints and solids for layers #2–#6. For layer #1 (the top layer), choose a solid, such as navy, black, or red. This layer, unslashed, becomes the yoke area and will be embellished, so a solid is most effective.

Use assorted braids, decorative threads, metallic or beaded appliqués (stars, anchors, or other nautical themes), trims, buttons, or beads for the yoke. Don't be afraid to use ribbons and braids that say "dry clean only." Metallic braids and cording, as well as metallic and embroidered ribbons that specify dry cleaning, have always worked well for me. I do suggest, however, that you run your completed sample block through the same washing and drying process that you will use for the finished jacket, to make sure it will be perfect.

Materials

Note: Do not prewash any of your fabrics.

YARDAGE REQUIREMENTS FOR CHENILLE LAYERS*				
Choose 5 fabrics (1 for each layer) for your size.				
Jacket Size	**42" to 45" wide**	**Total Yardage**	**58" to 60" wide**	**Total Yardage**
Petite	2¾ yds.	13¾ yds.	1⅞ yds.	9⅜ yds.
Small	2⅞ yds.	14⅜ yds.	2 yds.	10 yds.
Medium	2⅞ yds.	14⅜ yds.	2 yds.	10 yds.
Large	3 yds.	15 yds.	2⅛ yds.	10⅝ yds.
Extra large	3⅛ yds.	15⅝ yds.	2⅛ yds.	10⅝ yds.

**Yardage does not include fabric needed for sample blocks.*

YARDAGE REQUIREMENTS FOR BASE LAYER AND BINDING		
Jacket Size	**42" to 45" wide**	**58" to 60" wide**
Petite	3 yds.	2⅛ yds.
Small	3⅛ yds.	2¼ yds.
Medium	3⅛ yds.	2¼ yds.
Large	3¼ yds.	2⅜ yds.
Extra-large	3⅜ yds.	2⅜ yds.

Note: The jacket pattern includes a ⅝"-wide seam allowance for the shoulder and side seams. There is no seam allowance on the neck and lower edges of the jacket and sleeves; these edges will be bound.

Supplies

Refer to "General Supplies" on pages 6–7. In addition, you need:

- Thread that contrasts slightly with the top layer of fabric
- Bobbin thread that matches the base layer
- 2½ yds. of trim for each row you want to place around the yoke
- Optional embellishments, such as sequins, beads, buttons, or appliqués

Referring to "Preparing the Pattern" on page 46, make "The Captain in Chenille" pattern in your size. Trace and cut out an extra yoke pattern for the front and back.

Preparing the Layers

1. Make sample blocks from your selected fabrics, referring to "Sample Blocks" on pages 25–33. (See sample blocks for this jacket on page 26.) After you've finished the sample blocks and selected the layering order for your fabrics, make 1 more sample block, layering it identically to your chosen sample. For this block, instead of stitching in rows and cutting, experiment with any embroidery and trimmings you plan to use on the yoke. See the sample I made on page 50.
2. Cut the jacket pieces from each layer of fabric, referring to the cutting layout on page 70. With right sides up, number the layers from top (#1) to base (#6).

Tip

TO SAVE TIME, CUT 2 OR 3 LAYERS TOGETHER, BUT TAKE CARE THAT THE LAYERS DON'T SHIFT WHILE YOU CUT. SOME RAYONS ARE SLIPPERY, SO USE PLENTY OF PINS TO SECURE THE PATTERN TO THE FABRICS.

3. Place the base-fabric back piece, wrong side up, on your work table. Stack the remaining back pieces on the base piece, right side up, matching the order of your chosen sample block. Pin around the outside edges and randomly across the entire surface. Repeat for the jacket fronts.

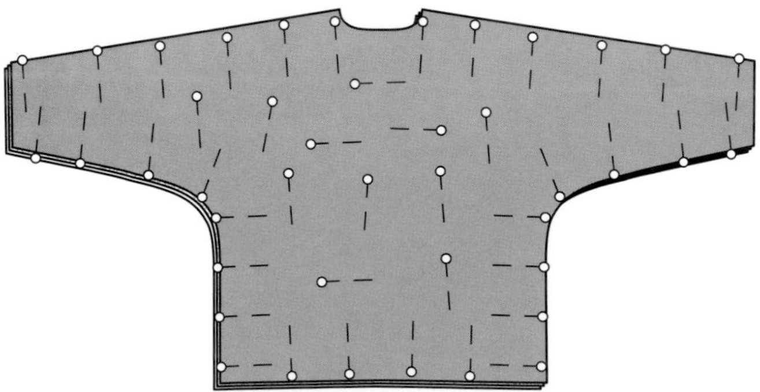

Note: Do not baste or sew the edges of your jacket layers in an attempt to keep everything lined up, and don't worry about the edges being perfectly even. The fabric layers will shift a little as you stitch, making the edges more uneven. Basting or sewing the edges together causes pleats and tucks to form as you stitch. After you've finished stitching and slashing, you'll trim the edges.

4. Place the extra yoke pattern on the top layer (#1) of the front and back. Using tailor's chalk or a marking pencil, mark the yoke. Set the stitch length on your machine at 10 to 12 stitches per inch. Stitch along the yoke line.

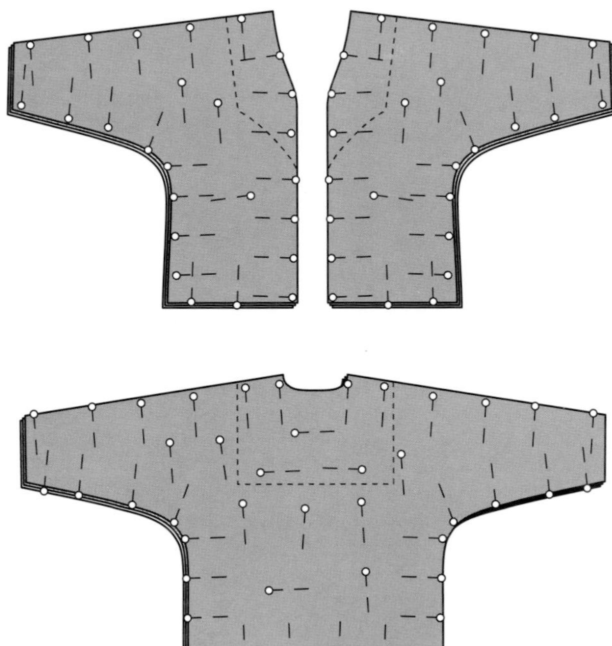

5. With layer #1 of the jacket front on top, place an acrylic ruler's 45°-angle line over the front edge as shown. Place the ruler so the line you draw will cut diagonally across the midsection of the jacket front. Move the pins if they are in the way of the ruler. Draw a line with tailor's chalk or a marking pencil to mark the first stitching line.

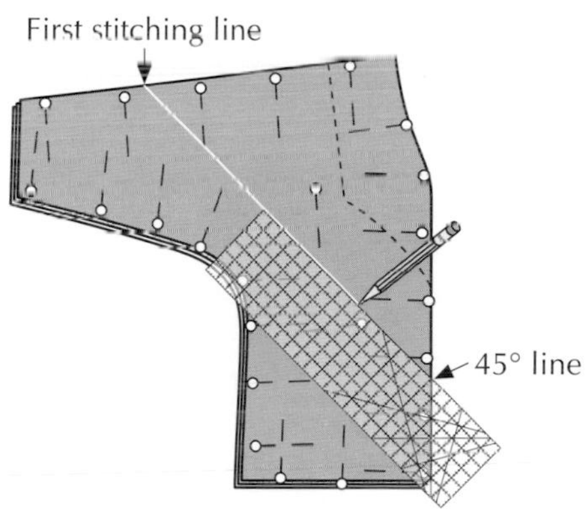

6. On the base fabric (layer #6), find the jacket back's center. The base layer will be the lining and the body of the jacket after the other layers have been cut, so determine the center back from this layer.

   Turn the jacket back over and on layer #1, draw a line down the jacket's center back from the yoke's stitching line to the lower edge.

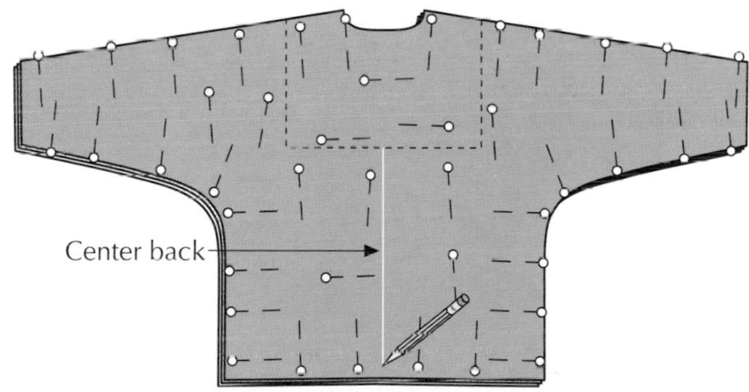

Note: *For this line, use a marking tool that won't rub off easily. You won't stitch on this line; you'll use it as a guide for pivoting the rows of stitching. After washing, the chenille will cover the line and it won't be visible.*

7. Place the ruler's 45°-angle line on the center-back line. Starting at the center-back line, draw the first half of the first stitching line. Turn the ruler over and place the 45°-angle line at the same place on the center-back line. Draw the second half of the first stitching line. The V that you've drawn becomes the basis for the jacket back's flattering chevron effect.

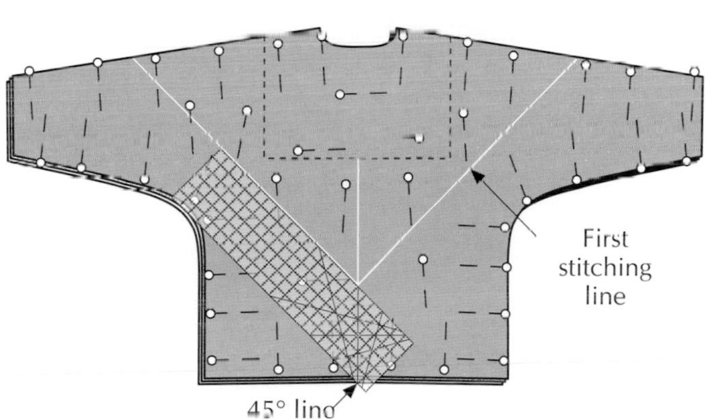

Stitching the Jacket Front

1. Starting at the center front on layer #1 of one jacket front, stitch on the line that you drew in step 5 of "Preparing the Layers." Sew to the shoulder, lift the presser foot, turn the jacket piece, then lower the presser foot ⅝" from the first row. Sew the second row from the shoulder to the center front, keeping the stitching line parallel to and ⅝" from the first row.

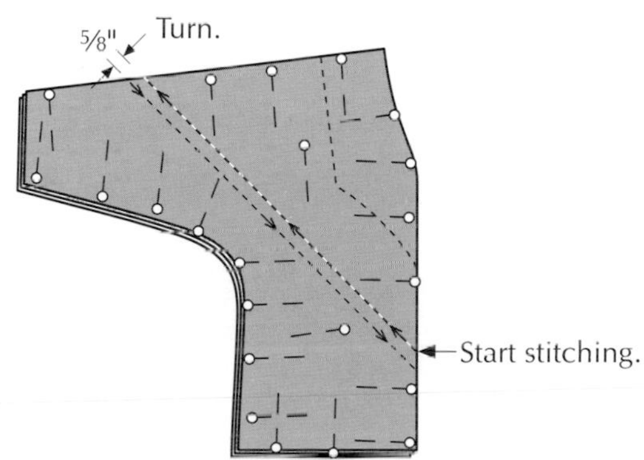

2. Continue stitching parallel rows and alternating directions until the jacket front is filled with stitching from the first row to the sleeves and lower edge. Be sure to maintain a 45° angle, with ⅝" between rows.

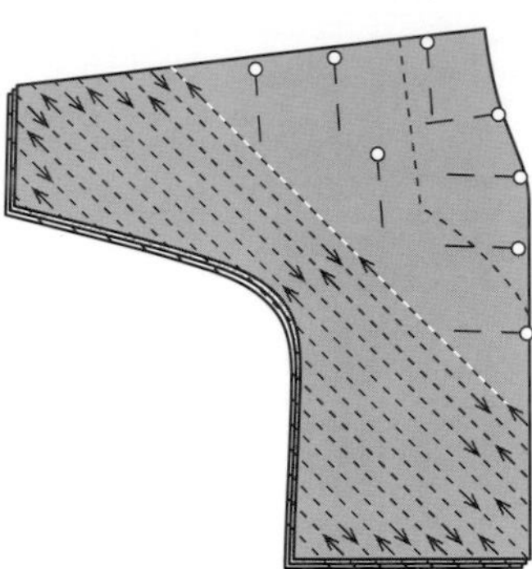

3. Stitch the rows on the other side of the first stitching line, alternating stitching directions and maintaining the ⅝"-wide spacing between rows. When stitching reaches the yoke line, backstitch the beginning and end of each row.

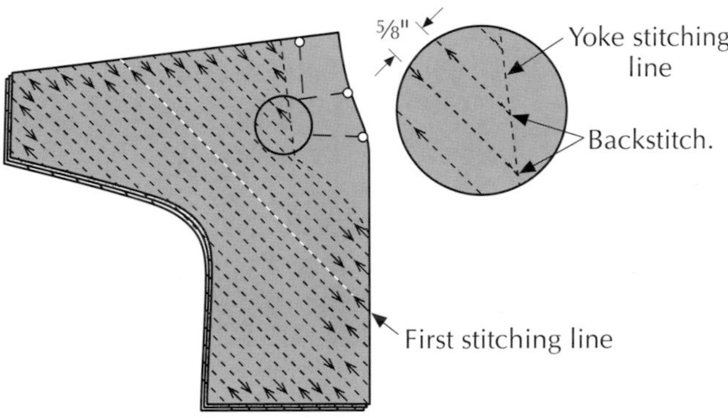

4. Repeat steps 1–3 for the second jacket front.

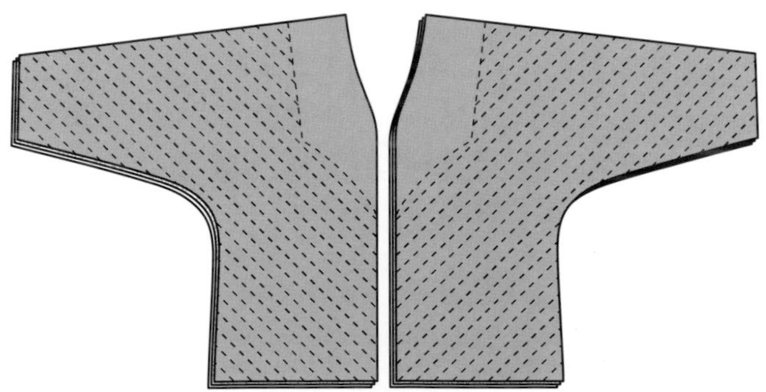

Stitching the Jacket Back

1. With the jacket back's layer #1 on top, stitch along the chevron line that you drew in step 7 of "Preparing the Layers." Starting at one shoulder, stitch to the point of the V at the center-back line. With the needle down, raise the presser foot, and pivot. Lower the presser foot and continue stitching to the other shoulder. Lift the presser foot, turn the jacket piece, then lower the presser foot ⅝" from the first row. Stitch the second row parallel to the first, pivoting again at the center mark.

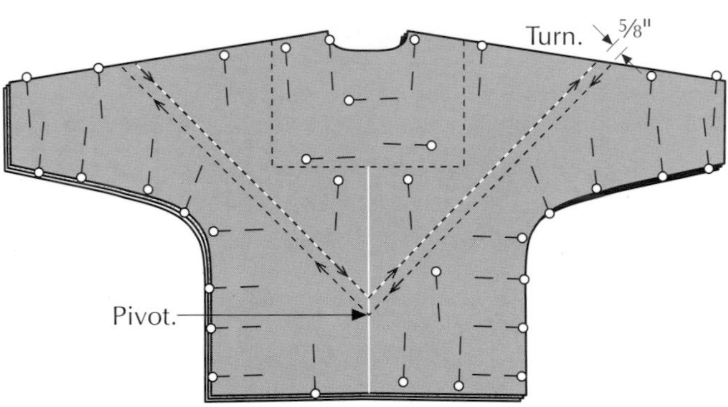

2. Continue sewing rows, alternating stitching directions, pivoting at the center line, and backstitching at the yoke, until the entire jacket back is filled with rows of stitching.

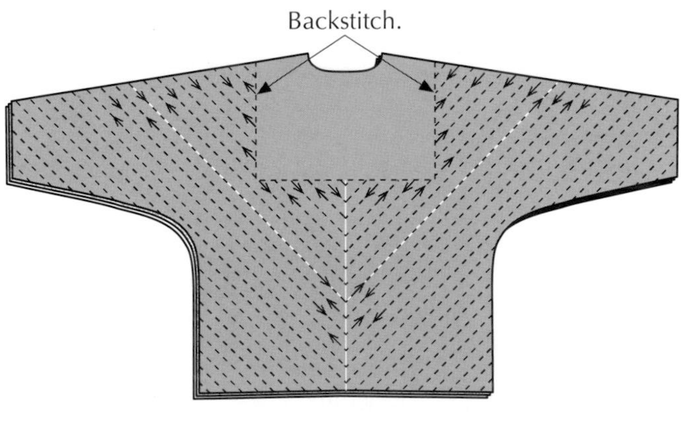

Note: *It is critical to be accurate when turning at the pivot point. If you are only 1 or 2 stitches to one side of the pivot point, the next row will be farther away from it, and after 3 or 4 rows, the chevron will change its angle. It's even possible to change the angle far enough from 45° that it affects the way the chenille blooms.*

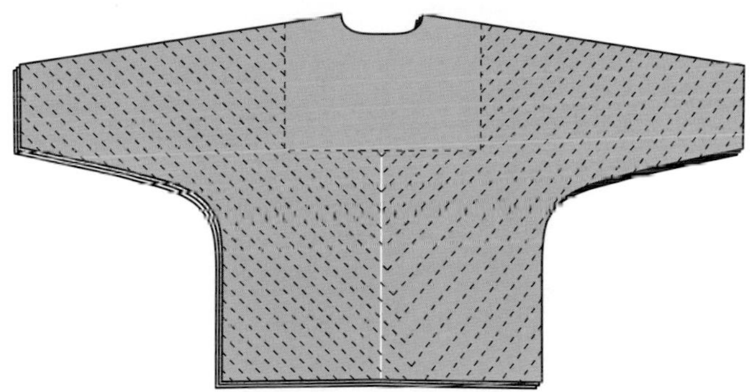

Even if you must adjust the spacing between rows in order to pivot at the correct point, the width of the rows will not show up after washing, but the angle of the chevron will.

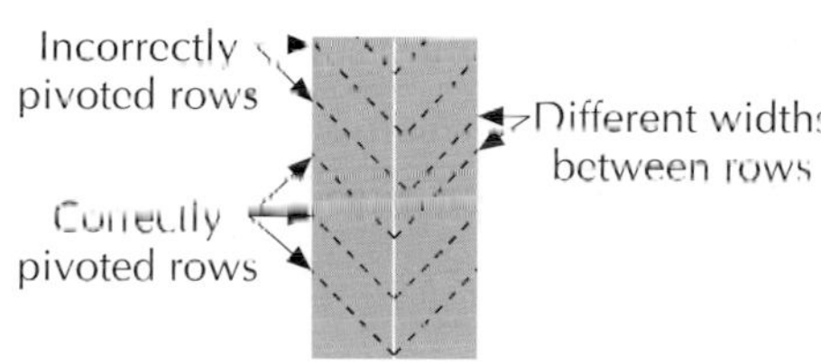

If the width between adjusted rows is less than ½" or greater than ¾", you need to remove stitches and resew to space the rows more evenly. (This is where the slight contrast between thread and layer #1 colors is helpful!)

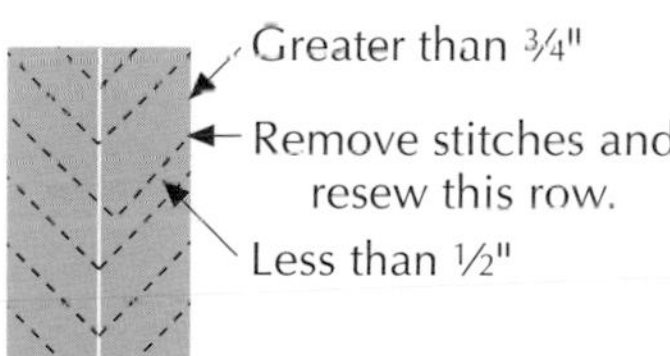

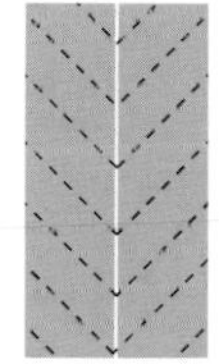

The quilted pieces are rather heavy, but don't be alarmed. After each step in the process, you'll find a change in the way the pieces feel and drape. Because the pieces move more freely after slashing, they seem lighter, and feel lighter yet after washing.

Slashing the Layers

1. Begin cutting rows from one edge of the jacket piece. Slip the lower blade of your scissors under the top 5 layers, sliding it over layer #6. Cut between the rows of stitching, along the middle, leaving about ¼" of fabric on each side of the stitched rows.

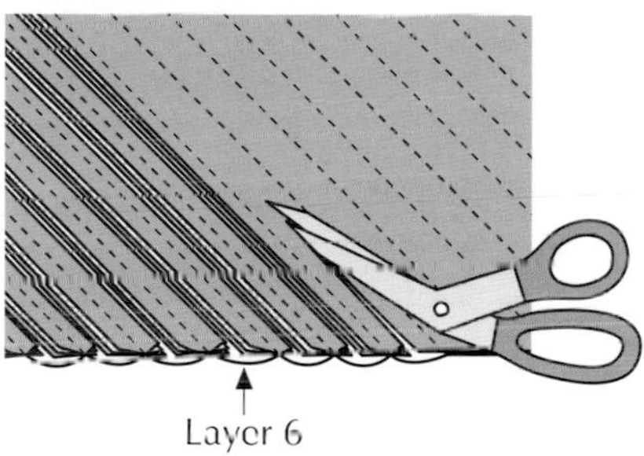

Note: *Take care not to cut or puncture the base layer. It's important that the base remain perfectly intact. This layer will be the main body of the jacket and will support all the chenille. If you accidentally cut it, however, it can be mended and secured. See "Mending Cuts and Holes" on pages 31–32.*

2. After you've cut all the rows, flip the pieces over. You'll see that as you stitched, the edges shifted, becoming more distorted and uneven than when you started.

3. Lay each jacket piece on a cutting mat, with the base-fabric side up. Place the pattern over the piece and, using a rotary cutter, trim the uneven edges. Carefully shift the cutting mat around the edges of the jacket and pattern as needed.

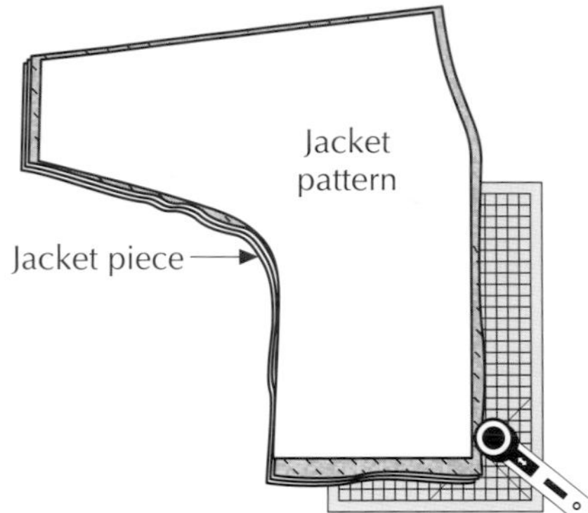

Note: *Do not trim the uneven layers until you've slashed all the rows. It's much easier to find the base layer and slip the blade of the scissors between the rows while the edges are uneven.*

Assembling the Jacket

1. With the base (lining) sides together and the slashed sides out, pin and stitch each jacket front to the back at the shoulders, using a ⅝"-wide seam allowance. Don't worry too much about matching slashes or stitching lines; minor differences won't show after you add the binding. Trim the seam allowances to ¼".

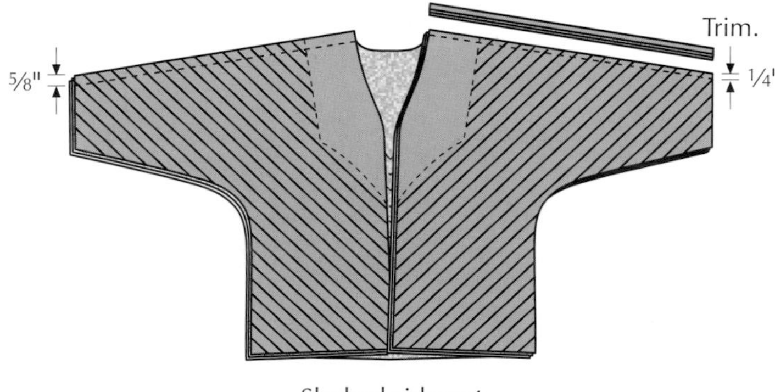

Slashed side out

Note: *When sewing construction seams with the slashed sides out, I find it helpful to use a popsicle stick or nail file to guide the cut edges and keep them flat as they pass under the presser foot.*

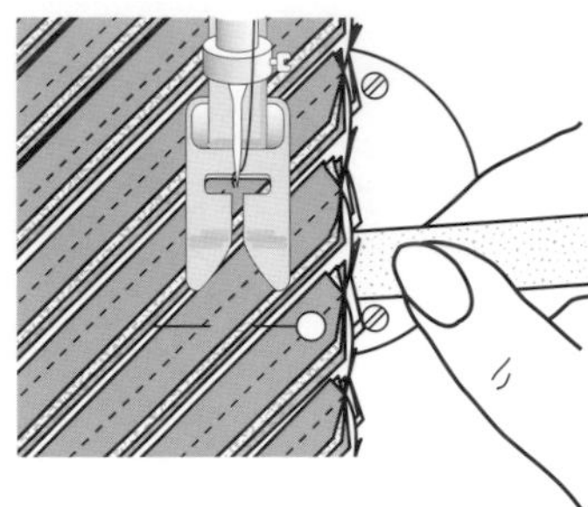

2. Open the jacket pieces and lay them flat across an ironing board, as you would when pressing open a seam.
3. Using as much steam as possible, press the seam allowance to one side as flat as you can. If the seam is too bulky to press to one side, place the iron on the seam and press, "mashing down" the seam allowances as much as possible and letting them go wherever they want. The idea is to get the seam allowances to lie as flat as possible.

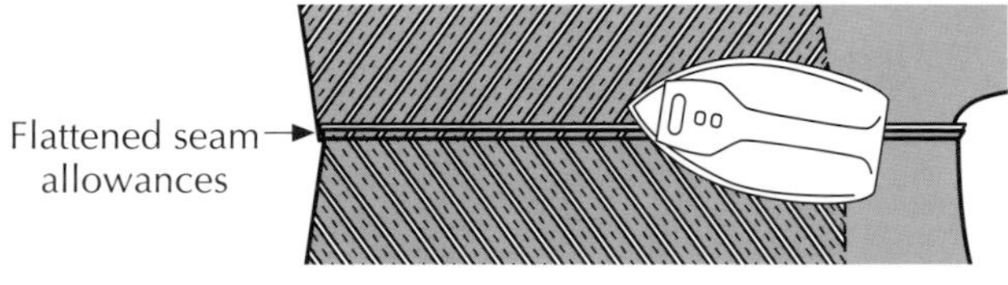

Press.

4. From layer #6 fabric, cut 2 bias strips, each 1¾" wide and the length of the shoulder seam plus 2". Press under the long edges so they meet in the center, or use a bias-tape maker to press and fold the strip.

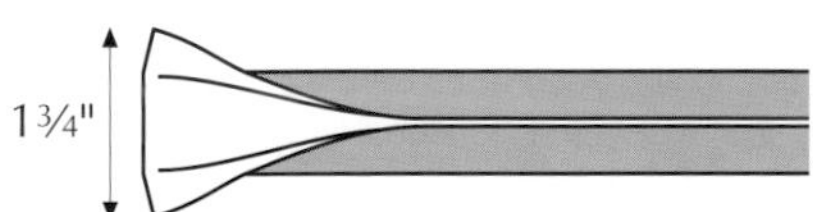

5. With the raw edges down, center the prepared bias strip over the shoulder seam and pin it in place. Stitch along one edge of the strip, close to the fold. Stitch the remaining edge.

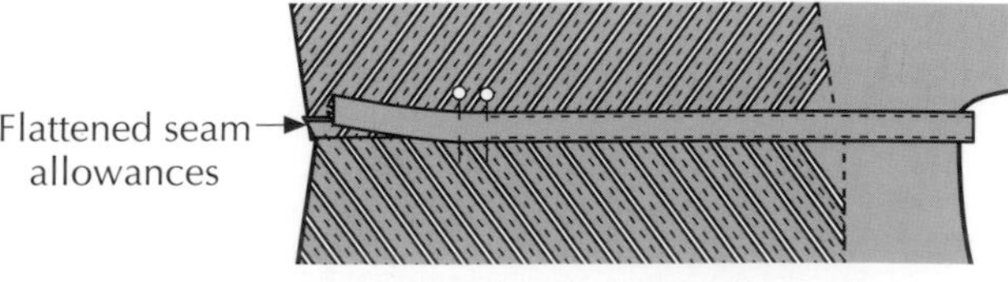

6. Pin the trim or braid to the edge of the yoke. Begin at the center front, cross the shoulder seam, continue around the back, and return to the center front on the other side in a continuous line. Stitch the trim to the jacket. (I like to use monofilament nylon in a narrow zigzag.) Add more trim in the same manner, but mark placement lines first for accurate spacing.

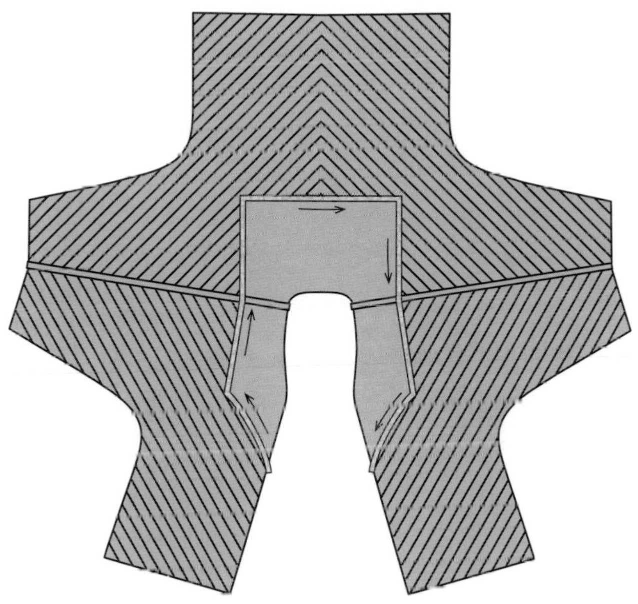

7. To prepare for embroidering the yoke, replace the regular presser foot with a darning foot and drop the feed dogs. Use decorative thread in the needle and thread that matches the lining in the bobbin.
8. To practice on a scrap, take 1 stitch and bring the bobbin thread to the top of the fabric. Holding both the upper and lower threads, begin stitching in a random pattern. Experiment. It's easy to maneuver a random, swirling, pattern—also called stipple quilting—from side to side and continue it into other rows.

   Even random quilting needs to be done in a pattern that is easy and natural for you to stitch. If the random stitching is uneven, with some rows of stitching close together and some far apart, the quilted layers won't lie flat. So play and create your own look. Here are a few ideas for stitching patterns.

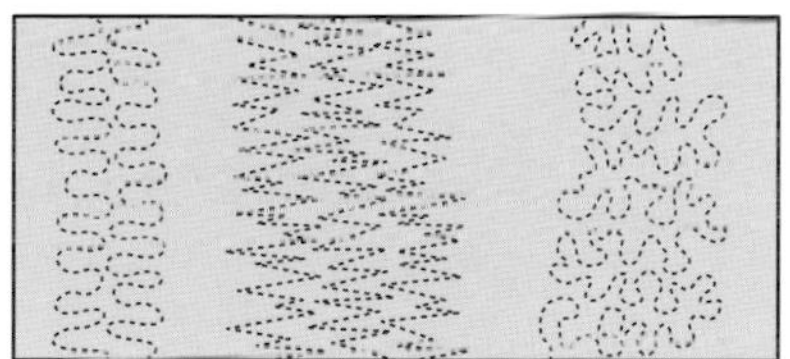

Tip

YOU MAY NEED TO ADJUST THE MACHINE'S TENSION TO GET A NICE STITCH. REDUCING THE TENSION SETTING BY ONE NUMBER IS GENERALLY ADEQUATE. BE SURE THE PRESSER FOOT IS LOWERED, OR THE TENSION WILL NOT WORK AT ALL.

IT IS POSSIBLE TO DO FREE-MOTION STITCHING WITHOUT A PRESSER FOOT, BUT IF MACHINE EMBROIDERY IS NEW TO YOU, YOU'LL PROBABLY BE MOST COMFORTABLE AND HAVE BETTER FIRST-TIME RESULTS USING THE DARNING FOOT.

9. Once you've developed your free-motion stitch, place the jacket flat on the sewing machine. Quilt the front and back yoke inside the rows of trims, leaving a ⅝"-wide margin along the neckline edge. I like my decorative stitching to show on the yoke area only, so I don't stitch into the binding area.

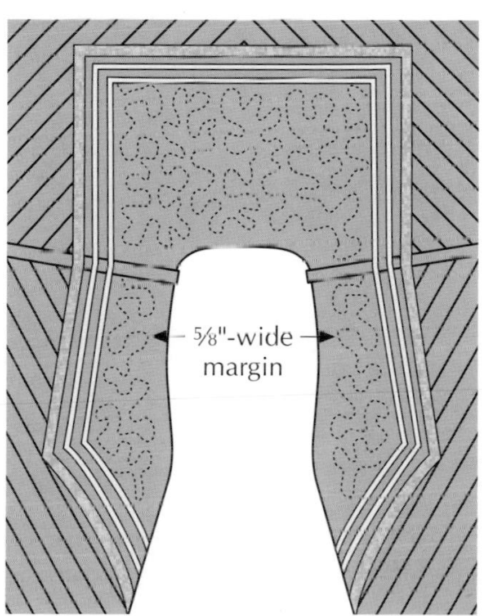

10. With the base (lining) sides together and the slashed sides of the jacket out, pin and stitch each underarm and side seam, using a ⅝"-wide seam allowance. Again, don't worry about matching slashes or stitching lines.

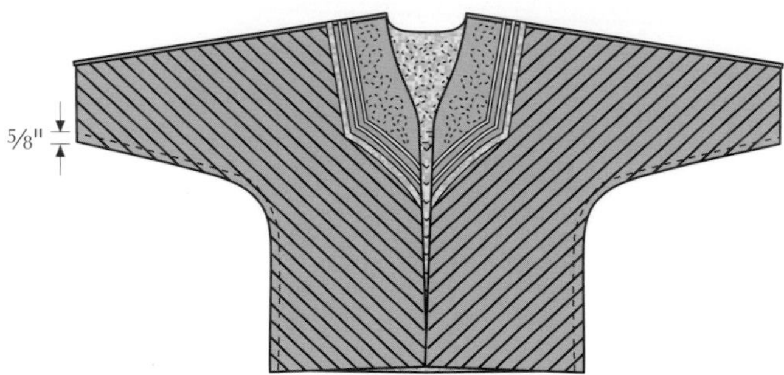

Note: *Fit the jacket at this point. Remember, it will shrink in size and length when washed, so it should fit more loosely than you want for the finished jacket. The sleeves should be at least 1" too long. If you fit the jacket as you normally would, it will be too small and the sleeves will be too short.*

11. Lay the jacket flat on the cutting mat. Using the rotary cutter, trim the seam allowances to ¼". Leave this seam unfinished to become part of the chenille when the jacket is washed.

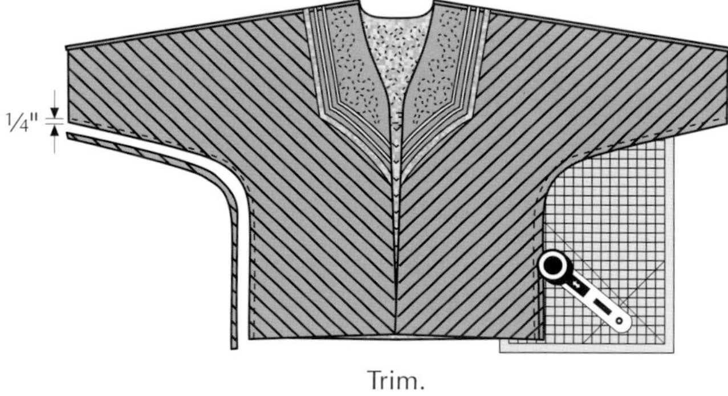

Binding the Jacket

1. From layer #1 fabric, cut 2¾"-wide bias strips for the binding. (To figure the width of the binding, multiply the desired finished width of the binding by 4, then add ¼".) Join the bias strips end to end until you have a strip long enough to go around the neck, front, sleeve, and lower edges of the jacket.

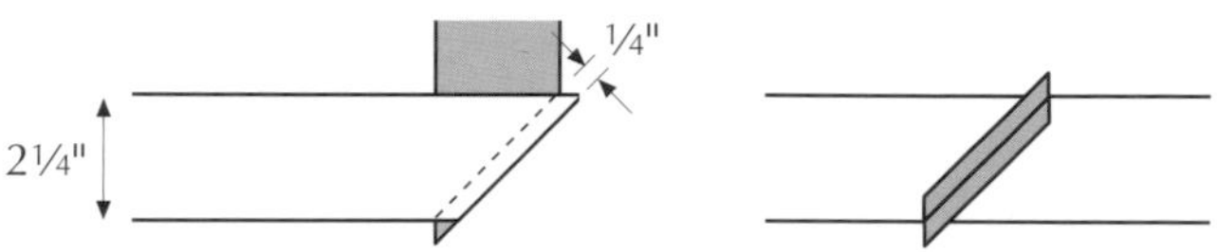

2. Beginning at one of the side seams at the bottom edge of the jacket, pin the *right* side of the bias strip to the *wrong* (lining) side of the jacket. Pin the binding around the entire unfinished outside edge of the jacket, mitering the corners. Pin the binding to the lower edge of each sleeve.

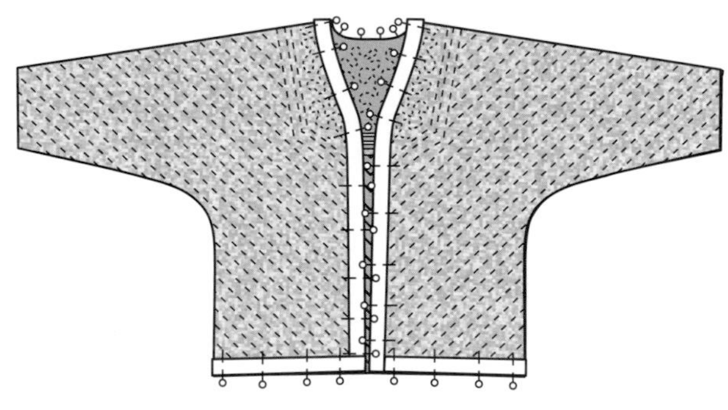

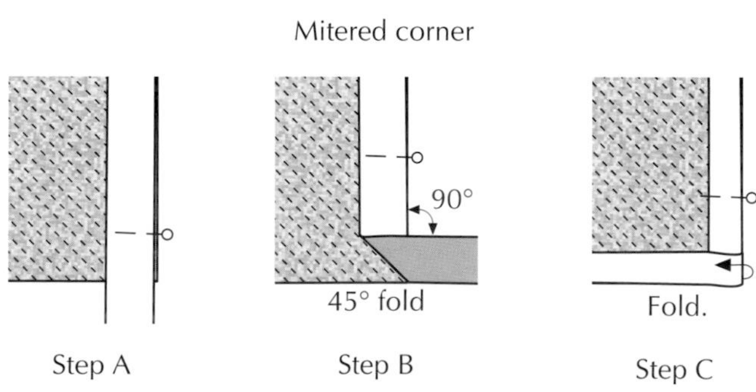

3. Overlap the binding ends at the side seam. Turn under the unfinished end of the bias strip that will be on top when the binding is turned to the right side.

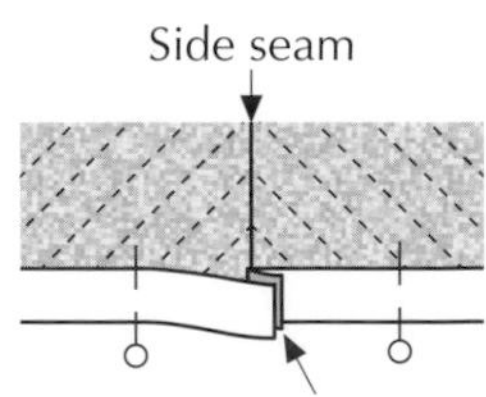

4. Stitch the binding to the jacket, using a ⅝"-wide seam allowance. At each corner, pull the fold of the binding away from the jacket and stitch to within ⅝" from the end. Remove the jacket from the machine and turn. Fold the binding back in place and begin stitching where the fold of the binding meets the jacket edge.

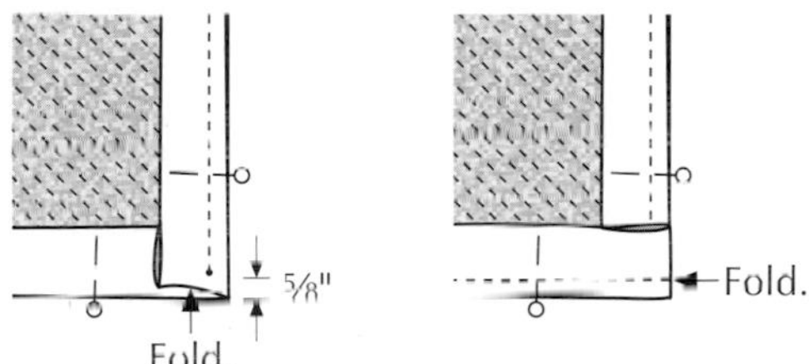

5. Turn the binding to the outside, folding it over the jacket edge. Turn under the edge and pin in place, using the stitching line as a guide.

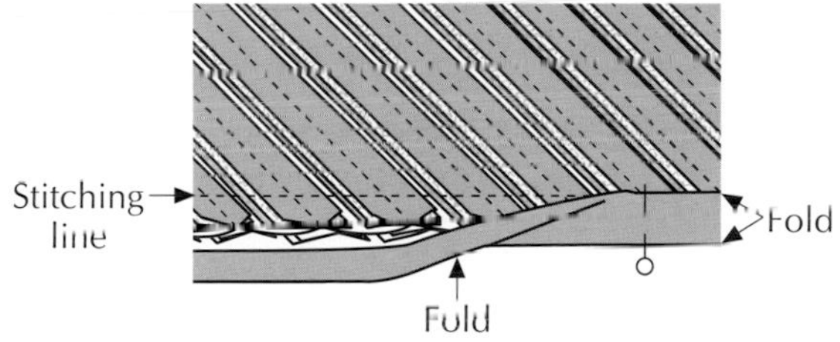

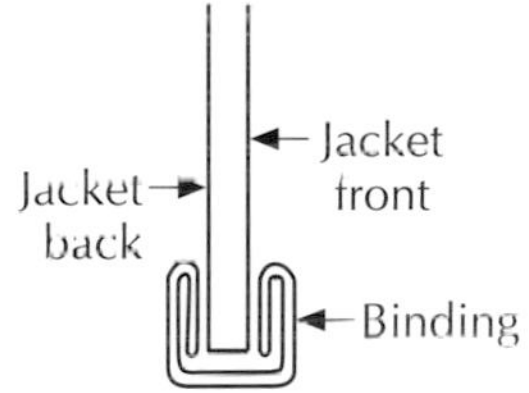

IF YOUR BIAS IS CUT FROM A SOFT, STRETCHY FABRIC, SUCH AS RAYON CHALLIS, SEWING IT TO THE INSIDE FIRST AND FINISHING IT ON THE OUTSIDE GIVES YOU MORE CONTROL OVER HOW THE BINDING LOOKS ON THE OUTSIDE. YOU CAN TURN UNDER THE EXACT AMOUNT NEEDED TO CREATE A PERFECT WIDTH FOR THE FINISHED EDGE AS YOU PIN THE BINDING IN PLACE.

IF YOUR BINDING SEEMS TOO SOFT AND IS HARD TO MANAGE, TRY APPLYING A LIGHT SPRAY STARCH AND PRESSING. THIS GIVES SOME BODY TO THE BIAS STRIP, MAKING IT EASIER TO HANDLE.

6. Edgestitch the inside fold of the binding, then edgestitch the outside fold. The stitching gives your binding a professional look and keeps it crisp and flat throughout the laundering process. Finish the bottom of the sleeve in the same manner.

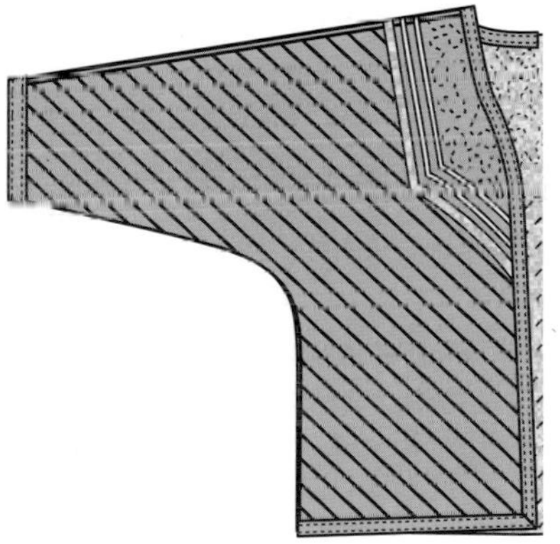

Finishing

1. Wash and dry your jacket, referring to "Laundering Chenille" on pages 32–33.
2. Add final embellishments to your jacket. Star appliqués, studs, or other decorative nautical embellishments are nice finishing touches.

Sawtooth Wall Hanging

DIMENSIONS: 42" x 42"

Color photo on page 52.

While making a coat for the 1996 Fairfield Fashion Show, I developed a technique that allowed me to apply my chenille ideas to quilting patterns. By cutting layered combinations into squares and then into triangles, I could place the chenille on a gridded base to create traditional quilt patterns. I found the idea of creating quilts and wall hangings with this soft, luxurious texture intriguing.

Developing the colorations was at first a challenge. When creating a palette for a garment, I work with fashion colors—colors that look great with everything from jeans to black silk. Colors for a wall hanging need to be home-decorating shades that complement a room and its accessories. So I must work with slightly different combinations for the home-decorating palette.

I chose the traditional Sawtooth pattern for this wall hanging. This design requires seven different colorations: six for the body of the wall hanging and one for the border. I developed each combination by making sample blocks the same way I do for garments. (See "Sample Blocks" on pages 25–33.) A challenge was finding enough fabrics: the solids, prints, and textures needed to make seven distinct colorations that blended well. Remember, however, that you can duplicate colors in the layered combinations.

I used rayons for the chenille layers and black 100% cotton for the base.

Fabric Selection

When choosing fabric, refer to the suggestions on pages 7–24. This project includes backing, batting, and base layers under the five slashed layers. For a wall hanging, select a heavy backing, such as cotton broadcloth or cotton twill, to give it body and stability. The batting—needlepunched cotton is ideal—and the base layer provide further support. For the base layer, use a fabric that is compatible with and similar to the five slashed layers.

Materials

Note. Do not prewash any of your fabrics.

Yardage Requirements*		
	42" to 45" wide	**58" to 60" wide**
Body of wall hanging	¼ yd. *each* of 15 fabrics	¼ yd. *each* of 15 fabrics
Base layer	2½ yds.	1⅜ yds.
Border layers	1⅛ yds. *each* of 5 fabrics	1 yd. *each* of 5 fabrics
Backing and binding	2¾ yds.	1½ yds.

**Yardage does not include fabric needed for sample blocks.*

Supplies

Refer to "General Supplies" on pages 6–7. In addition, you need:

- Thread that contrasts slightly with the top layer of fabric
- Bobbin thread that matches the base layer
- 1 piece of cardboard, approximately 17" x 20", for each chenille coloration
- 46" x 46" piece of needlepunched cotton batting

Assembly

1. Make sample blocks for each of the different colorations you'll use in the project. (See "Sample Blocks" on pages 25–33.) I used 6 colorations for the body and 1 additional coloration for the border.
2. Cut backing, batting, and base layers 46" x 46" (2" larger than the finished size on each side). If needed, cut the backing and base fabric in half crosswise, then sew the halves together lengthwise to make pieces wide enough. Place the base layer on the batting, right side up, then place both layers on the backing, which should be right side down. Pin the edges together.

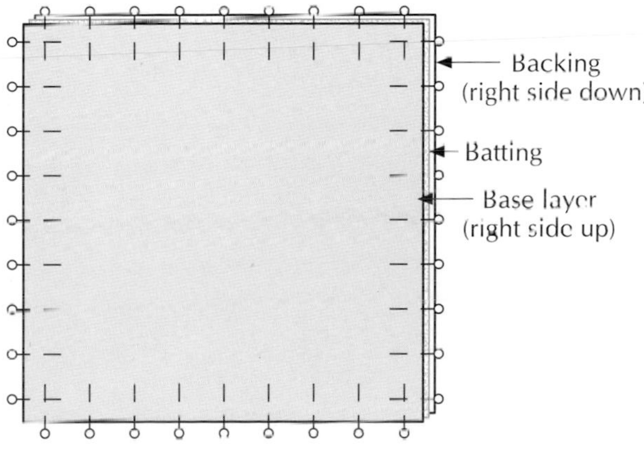

3. Using an acrylic ruler and a marker, draw a line on the base layer 2" from each edge to mark the finished size. Draw a second line 3" inside the first for the borders. Move the pins if they are in the way of the ruler. Draw a 12 x 12–square grid inside the second line, each square measuring 3" x 3". The grid is your placement guide.

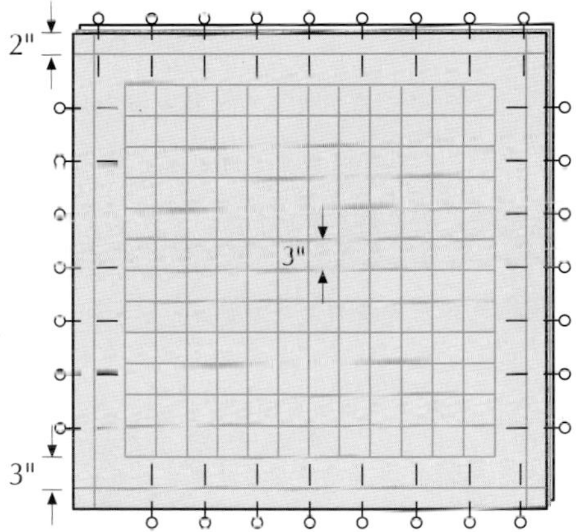

4. Stack the fabrics, of each coloration, for the body of the wall hanging, matching the chosen order of your sample blocks. Cut each stack into 6 squares, each 6" x 6", for a total of 36 stacked squares.

5. With a rotary cutter, cut each stacked square in half vertically, and without moving the pieces, cut the block in half again horizontally. Each resulting stacked square will be 3" x 3". Without disturbing the cut block, cut it twice diagonally to make 8 triangle stacks. You will have a total of 288 triangle stacks. Before moving them, pin each triangle stack securely to keep the layers from shifting.

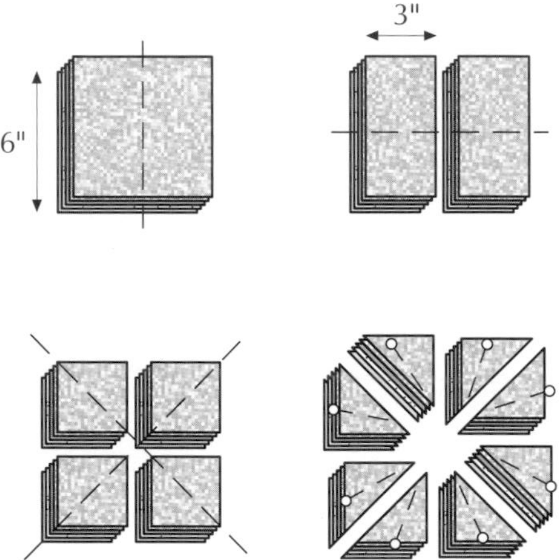

6. Place the triangle stacks on the pieces of cardboard, each coloration on a separate piece. Stack the triangles evenly, overlapping the point of one stack with the straight edge of the next.

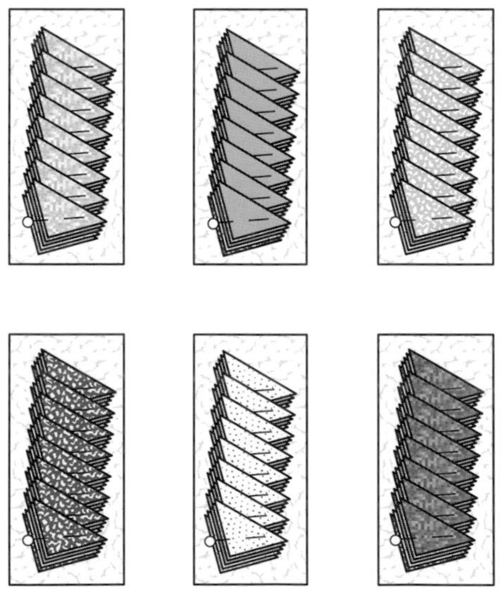

7. Place the triangle stacks on the grid in a traditional Sawtooth pattern as shown, leaving a 3"-wide margin clear on all 4 sides for the border. Change the colorations from row to row. Pin all 3 points of each triangle stack in place to make it easier to keep the pattern sharp. Continue placing stacks until all the grid squares are filled with triangles.

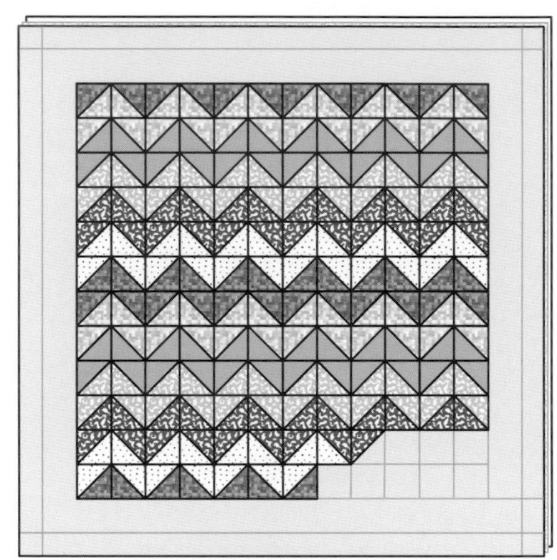

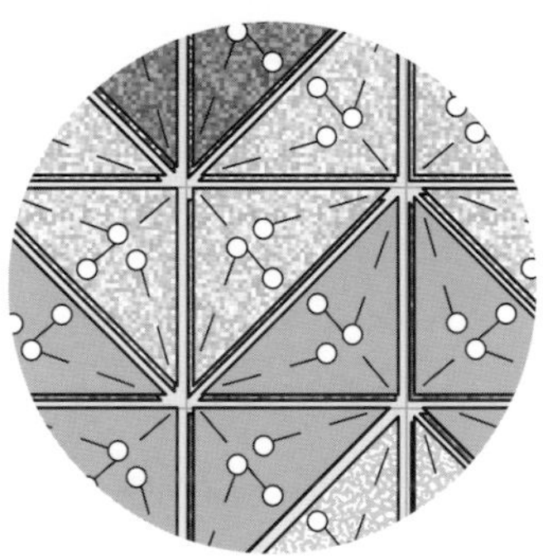

8. Layer the 5 border fabrics, matching the order of your chosen sample block. Pin the edges to keep the fabrics together. Align the 45°-angle line of a Bias Square ruler with one edge of the stack. Slide a long ruler along the edge of the Bias Square. Draw a 45°-angle line across the stack.

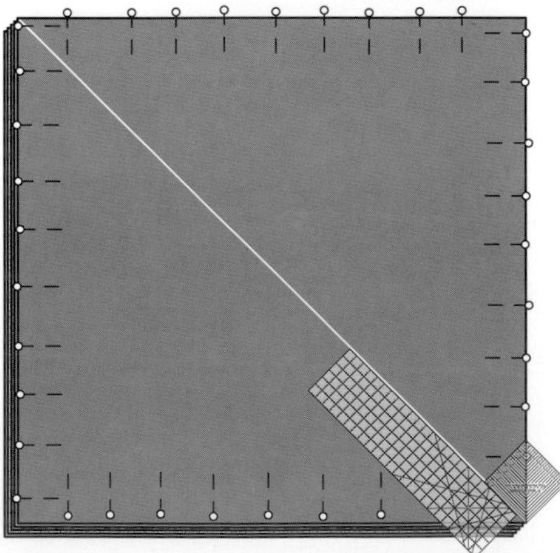

9. Cut along the line with a rotary cutter. Taking care to avoid the pins, cut 2 strips, each 3" wide, from each side of the first cut for a total of 4 strips. Cut extra border strips later as necessary.

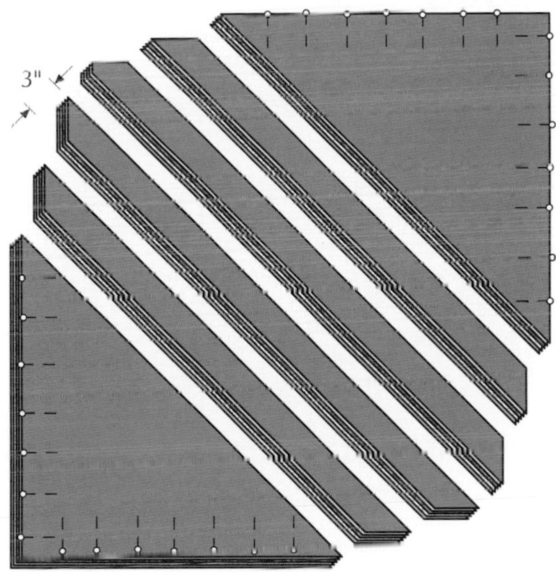

10. Place the angled ends of the 3"-wide strips at the corners of the grid. To join sections or fill in any spaces along the border, cut straight across the 3"-wide strips where they will join and butt the ends. Pin the border pieces in place, making sure the edges and ends are securely fastened.

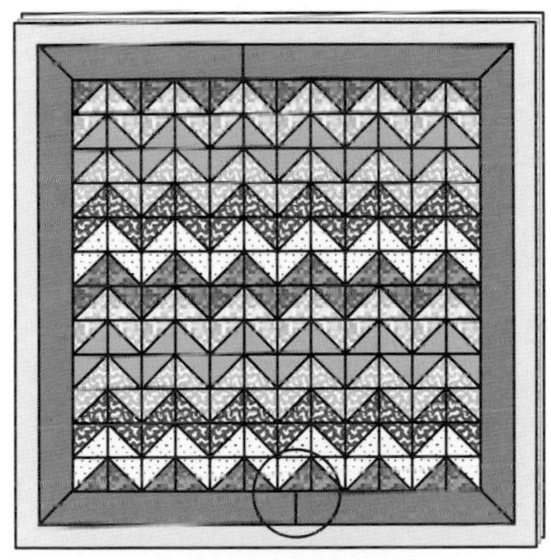

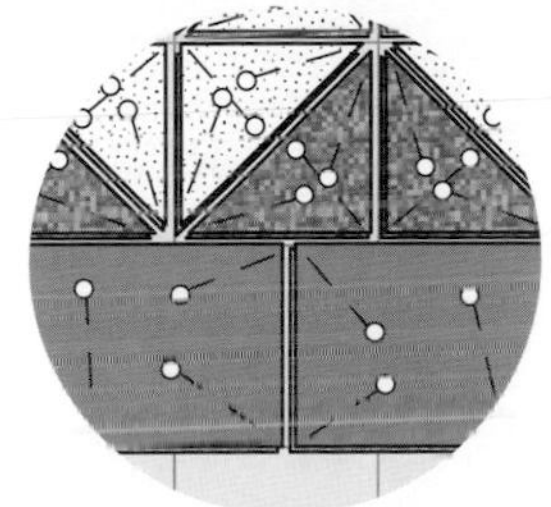

11. On the body of the wall hanging, draw 2 parallel stitching lines, each ⅜" from the edge of each Sawtooth coloration. Draw a third stitching line between these two lines, approximately ⅝" from each.

Note: It is critical that the points of the triangles are secured, so be sure that your stitching lines cross close to the points as shown.

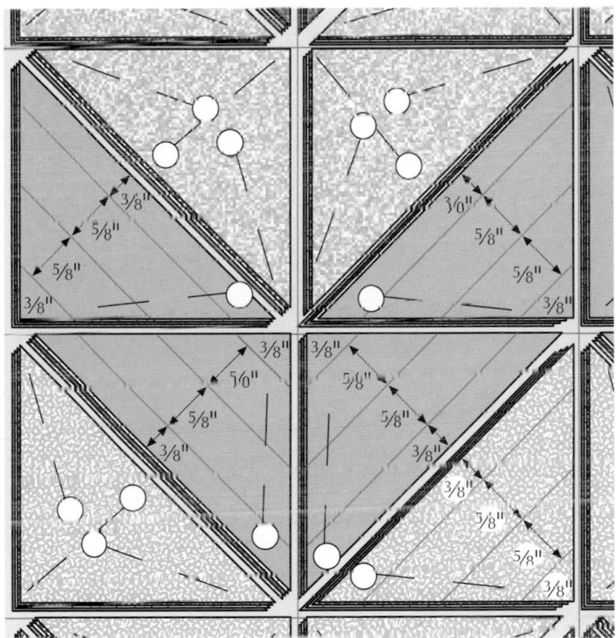

12. On the border, draw a stitching line ⅜" from the body of the wall hanging. Draw 3 more stitching lines parallel to the first, each ⅝" apart. The third line will be ¾" from the edge.

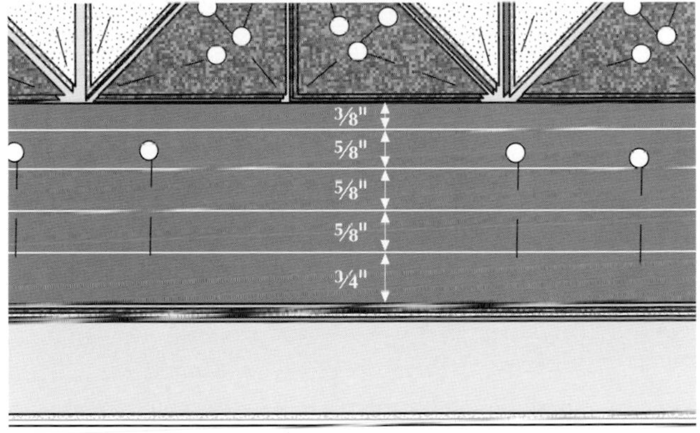

Note: The border of the wall hanging shown on pages 52 and 80 is cut along the grain line and stitched and slashed in a diagonal pattern. After laundering this piece, there were so many exposed ends, I was concerned they wouldn't hold up well to handling. Border strips cut on the bias, then slashed parallel to the edges of the wall hanging, provide a more secure design. If you're daring, experiment with the borders to make your own design.

13. Stitch along the drawn lines in the Sawtooth and border areas, backstitching at the beginning and end of each row. Pull the threads up to the top of the work and knot them securely to keep them—and the points of the triangles—from working loose during washing. Trim the thread ends to about ⅜"; they will disappear in the bloom of the chenille.

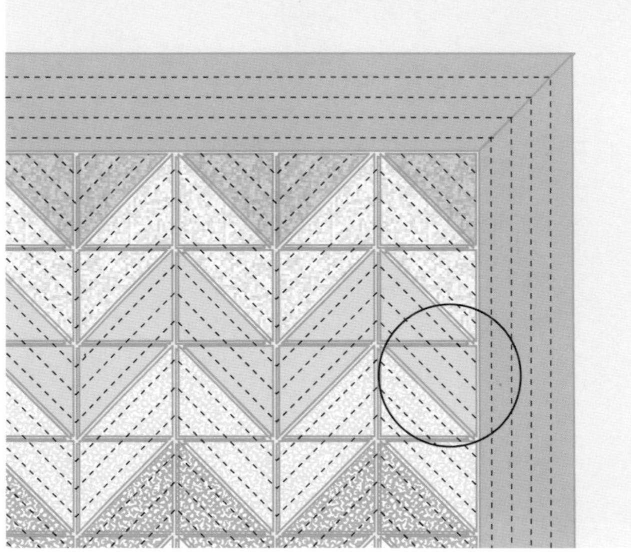

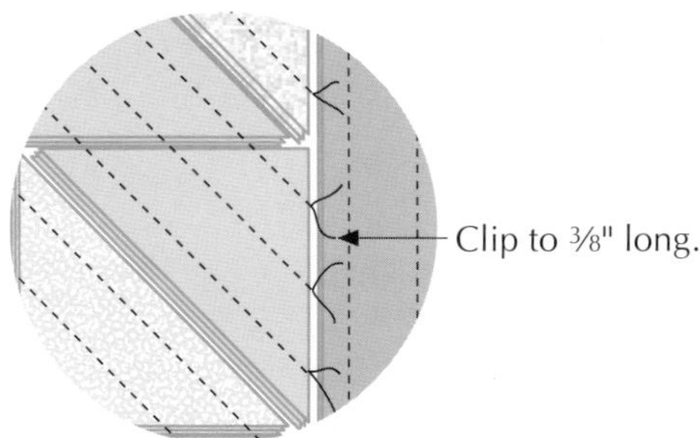

14. After stitching all the rows, cut the top 5 triangle and border layers between the rows of stitching. Do not cut into the bottom 3 layers (base fabric, batting, and backing).

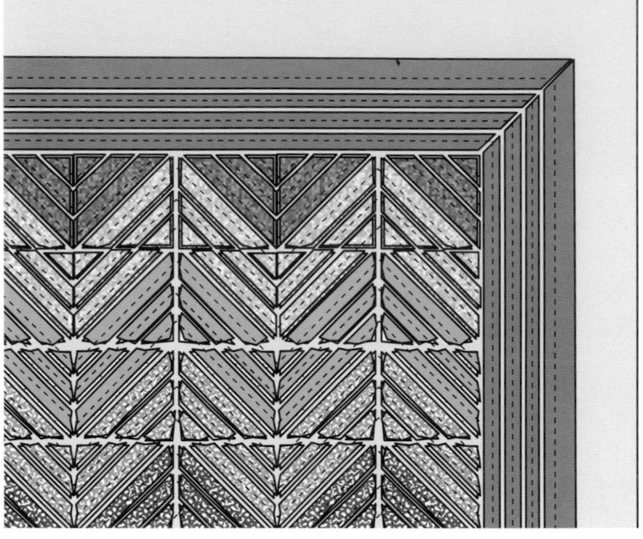

Slash.

Note: If you used a needlepunched cotton batting, you can make the batting part of the cut layers. Either cut the batting and base layer between all the layers, or cut patterns in all the layers in some areas and leave some of the base and batting intact in other areas.

15. When all the rows have been cut, trim the excess fabric and batting that extend beyond the border.

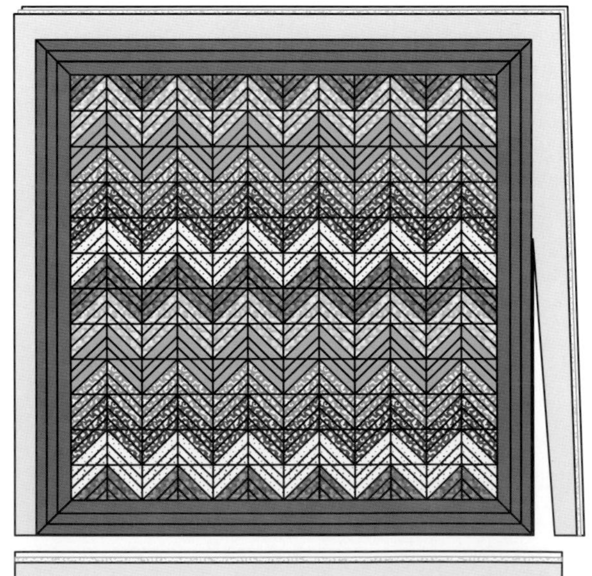

Trim.

16. Fold the quilt in half crosswise, lining up the edges. Check to see that the widths at the top and bottom of the quilt are equal. Fold the quilt in half lengthwise to check the lengths of the sides. Place a Bias Square ruler at each corner and trim to square the quilt. If the widths don't match, or if the lengths are not the same, trim carefully as needed.

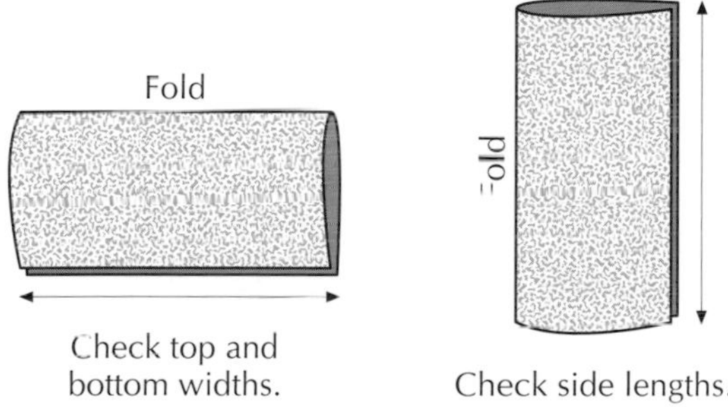

Check top and bottom widths. Check side lengths.

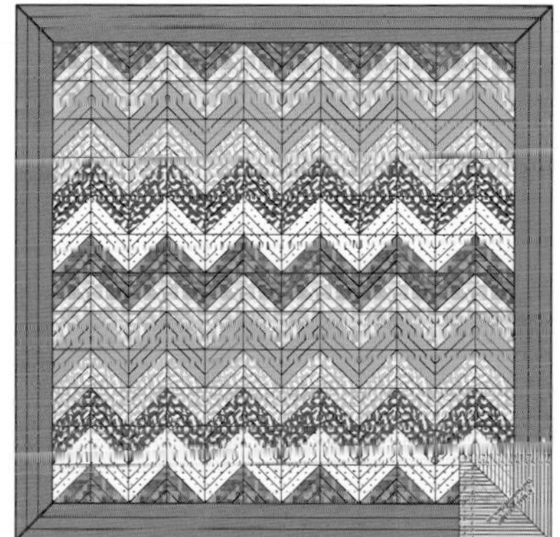
Trim as needed.

Adding Binding

1. From the binding fabric, prepare enough 2¾"-wide bias strips to go around the perimeter of the wall hanging (overlap each end by 4" when measuring). Join the strips end to end.
2. Pin the binding to the quilt, placing right sides together and matching raw edges. Starting 4" from the end of the binding, stitch through all layers, ⅝" from the raw edges. Miter the corners, referring to step 2 of "Binding the Jacket" on page 78.

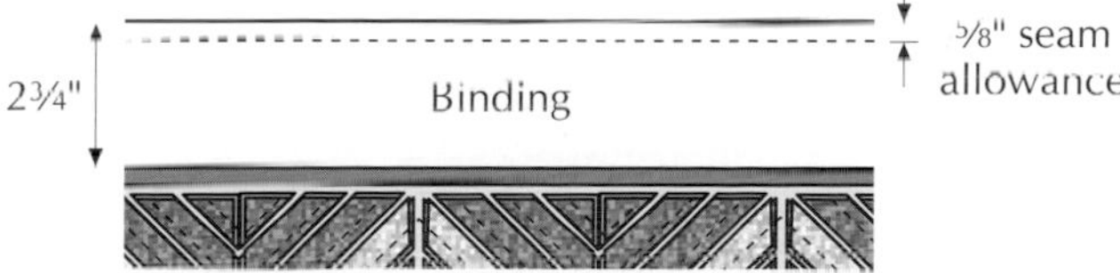

3. Stitch to within 4" of the end of the binding strip. Remove the quilt from the machine, then cut and join the ends of the binding at a 45° angle. Sew the remaining binding to the quilt.

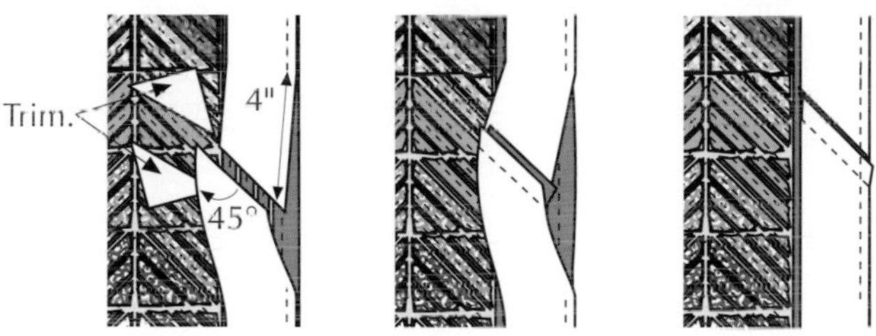

4. Fold the binding to the back of the quilt. Turn the raw edge under ⅝" and stitch it to the back of the quilt.

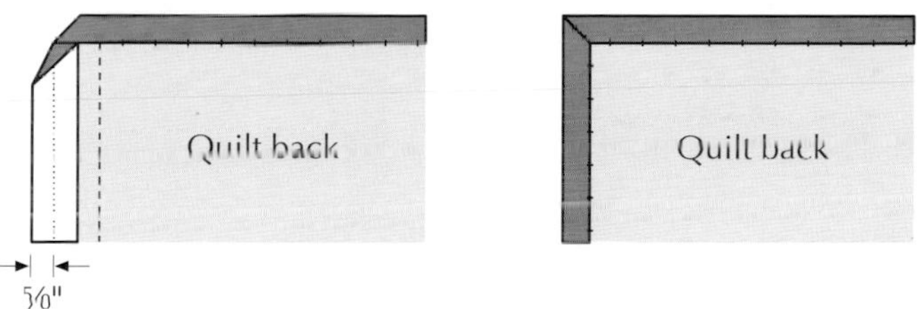

5. The wall hanging is now complete and ready to be washed and dried. Refer to "Laundering Chenille" on pages 32–33 for directions.

You've created a wall hanging that has beautiful texture, depth, and color. Use the methods for this project to create original patterns. If you keep the basic guidelines in mind as you create your design and choose stitching directions, the possibilities will be endless.

The Puzzler

33" x 28"

Color photo on page 52.

Materials

Yardage does not include fabric needed for sample blocks.

6 rectangles, *each* 39" x 44", for pink coloration
6 rectangles, *each* 27" x 29", for blue coloration
6 rectangles, *each* 25" x 28", for orange coloration
1 rectangle, 32" x 37", for backing
1 rectangle, 32" x 37", of batting
½ yd. of 42"- to 60"-wide fabric for binding

1. On a large sheet of paper (or several small sheets taped together), draw a 28" x 33" rectangle. Draw a dot at each corner, 3" from the long side and 7" from the short side.

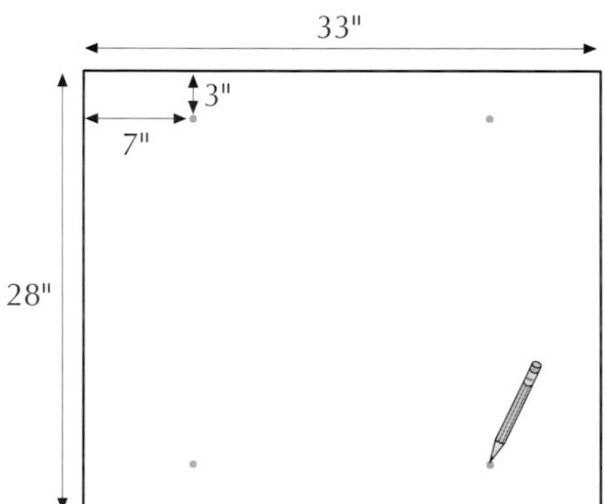

2. Using a protractor or a string tied to a pencil as shown, draw 4 intersecting arcs, each with a radius of 20"; use the dots you drew in step 1 as the center of each partial circle.

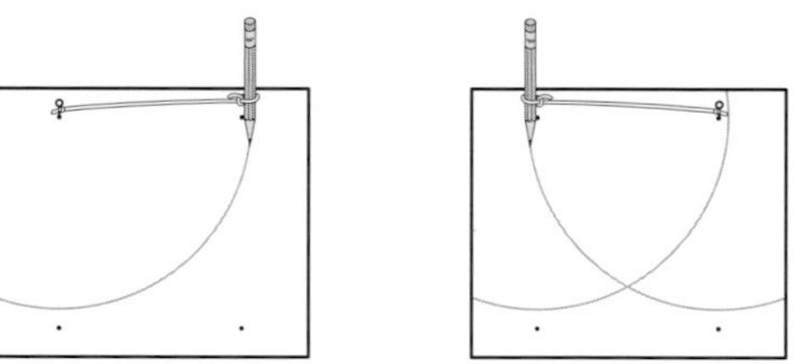

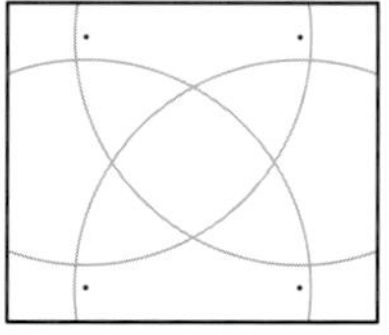

3. Number the sections and note the desired coloration and stitching orientation of each section. Cut the pattern apart, or, using the pattern as a master, trace, mark, and cut out the sections to use as templates.

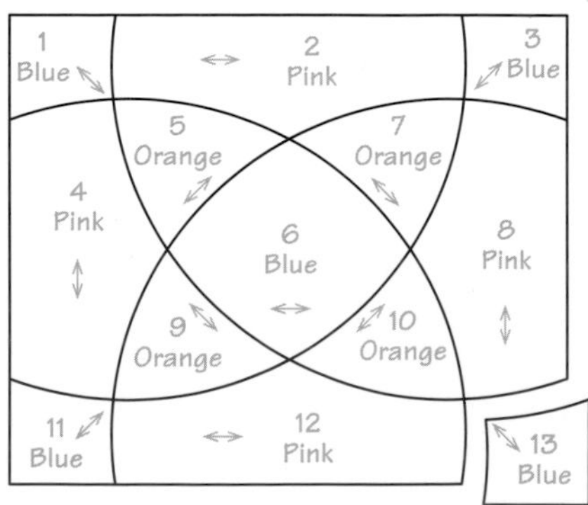